Endorsements

Let's break through the glass ceilings in our professional lives, and see our roles in the marketplace from a better vantage point. Heaven's.

Think, Speak, Live, Business from Heaven's Perspective will help you to bridge the gap between your professional career and your Christian faith, as Pastor Mark Appleyard shares practical tools that will deepen your understanding of important spiritual principles, dramatically impacting the way you approach professional life.

With simple but powerful insights, *Think, Speak, Live, Business from Heaven's Perspective*, will be an asset to any Christian business-person who is wanting to succeed... in EVERY area of life.

Hamish Hargreaves
Dubai UAE
Cox Architecture
Associate - BArch(Hons)
RAIA LEED GA Estidama PQP

Pastor Mark Appleyard writes a very straightforward, to the point, but challenging book, that will make you re-think how you operate in your work and indeed your private or homely environment. In fact, this compartmentalized approach to life, which seems so natural to most of us, is actually a great inhibitor to allowing us to access our full, divinely given potential, and release it for the benefit of not only us, but for everybody we encounter. Useful tools are there to help guide us and are unique to Mark's work.

These will be helpful to anybody, especially to all of us in business who have a tendency to apply one set of rules to operate in one artificial compartment of life, say your private life and one set in your business life.

Toby Baxendale
United Kingdom
Entrepreneur/Investor

Mark Appleyard is a friend, a man of faith and grace. He is humble and unafraid. It's this combination that has given him great access to heaven's perspective. *Think, Speak, Live* is a clearly written directive for living out the mandate Jesus gave us, "On earth as it is in heaven."

Mark is concise and generous in his teaching. Like all great communicators, he balances story with application. *Think, Speak, Live*, is both an impartation and a practical step by step instruction. While the book is directed toward business leaders, every believer would benefit from the wisdom in its pages. If you desire to know better how God thinks and speaks, if your passion is to live His Kingdom come, I recommend this book.

Jason Clark
North Carolina
Director of A Family Story Ministries
Author of, *Prone To Love, God Is (Not) In Control, & Untamed*

How would you like a personal guide to walk you into a greater integration of your spiritual life with your daily activities? *Think, Speak, Live* is just that. I have been a follower of Christ in business for more than 20 years and yet after incorporating just one chapter of this book I found my confidence in connecting and communicating with God jumped up TEN FOLD.

I wish I had access to this 20 years ago! Don't hesitate to grab your copy and get activated to *Think, Speak, and Live* from heaven's perspective in your personal and business life NOW.

Andy Mason
California USA
Director of Heaven in Business
Author of, *Dream Culture: Bringing Dreams to Life and God with You at Work*

I have had the privilege of doing life and ministry with Mark and Julie for the past eight years. There is no one I have ever known who has a greater passion for equipping Christian business leaders to become world changers than Mark Appleyard, nor have I ever met anyone who is more effective in doing so.

In *Think, Speak, Live*, Mark gives, pragmatic, real world, helpful, useful tools and strategies for transforming our life's perspective and world view in order to impact our spheres of influence. As such, *Think, Speak, Live* is nothing short of a must read for those who, as the title says, want to live their life from heaven's perspective.

Lowell McNaney
North Carolina USA
Senior Pastor Crossroads United Methodist Church
Author of, *Fuel for the Journey*

Mark Appleyard is an inspiration to me and a man who offers much encouragement into my everyday life as a doctor and church leader. He has learnt lessons in the journey of life that we can all learn from, and in *Think, Speak, Live*, Mark shares what he has learnt en route, with illustrations from life as the colorful background.

Great truths about who God is and who he has made us to be light up the pages, thoughts such as *Position and Potential*, challenge and stimulate, and then practical ideas help us apply these truths to life itself. Read and be inspired.

Dr. Pete Carter MD
United Kingdom
Medical Doctor
Director of Eastgate and its Healing Centre
(www.eastgate.org.uk)
Author of, *Unwrapping Lazarus*

Who would have thought that God would be able to impart such spiritual wisdom through engaging stories and clear practical leadership principles to business entrepreneurs and executives, from an Australian electrician, turned pastor? In thoughtful bite-sized chunks, Mark urges and woos us as leaders to go deeper into a Trinitarian God of power, relevance and purpose. We would do well to follow him there!

Doug Balfour
Philadelphia USA
CEO Geneva Global
Author of, *Doing Good Great: An Insider's Guide to Getting the*
Most Out of Your Philanthropic Journey

Anothen Business Series
THINK SPEAK LIVE BUSINESS FROM HEAVEN'S PERSPECTIVE

Cover design by Keira Prowd, Prowd Design
Author's Photo by Whitney Gray,
www.whitneygrayphotography.com
Web development Legacy Creative, www.legacycreative.co
Book Formatting by Reddovedesign.com

ISBN – 978-1-946503-02-2

To order more books or resources,
or to enquire about consulting or speaking engagements
visit: www.anothen.co

Dedication

THIS BOOK IS DEDICATED TO MY MUM AND DAD

You modelled to me that you can give more with a smile than a checkbook. You revealed to me that every person has value. You exposed me to a love that knows no bounds.

Although many years have passed since you transitioned from this world to the next, and your physical memorial lay thousands of miles from where I am, your legacy of life, love and laughter remain part of me always.

Thank you for giving me life and belief.

I love you.

Table of Contents

Acknowledgements

A mentor of mine once quipped how for two thousand years there have been millions of believers who have had billions of thoughts about God. His point? It is nearly impossible to truly have an original thought about Him.

And so, I find it appropriate to honor the many people who have taken the already well considered ideas and pondered thought from ages past, and spent hours with me to wrestle them into contemporary expression, mixed with the fresh revelation of our always perfect Father.

As I reflect, names such as Russel Hinds, S. Ed Hoard, CJ (Joey) Huggins and Bill Joukhadar come to mind. Four very different men of God who provided me with the basic foundations of Christian leadership experience. These men provided me with leadership vocabulary that became the echo for my newly forming leadership voice to practice upon.

People such as Constantine Giovas, a person whose use of his shepherding gifts released in me a compassion for people that has repositioned the rhythms of my heart to beat in time with my heavenly Fathers'. And Rob Buckingham, whose raw and honest approach to the Spirit filled life, gave me the courage and permission to take steps into the spiritual waters that my paradigm had previously held me back from.

Then there is Beth McCormack… A small statured and aged woman of God with the faith of a giant. An inspirational life, lived out quietly before me in the shadows of a crazy world.

And what about Lowell and Jennifer McNaney? These two incredible people of God saw in me what others did not. They elevated me to a place of influence from a place of relative obscurity. They revealed to me the power of belief in people.

Jason Clark is a dear friend and theological thinker, who has continued to shower me with the grace to walk out on the theological edge and dare to look over to see the face of God. His heart for us, particularly on this project, has been transformational.

Our Crossroads family and leadership, have continuously put down the metrics of natural church culture and pursued the metrics of heaven at great cost, in a bid to do whatever it takes to bring people into a transformational encounter with the living God. There encouragement and editing prowess have helped transform abstract thought into practical living.

There is Mark and Katherine Stoleson, who humbly do their best to live out the very principles I discuss in this book and who have proven to me that the world can indeed be changed for the glory of our always good God.

And my beautiful bride, Julie, and our three amazing kids, Dane, Jessie-Naree and Alex-Anne. These are the true people of legendary faith. People whose love for Jesus is just crazy enough to follow me quite literally to the ends of the earth. People who have sacrificed and given up all to live a life, as Paul says in Ephesians four, *"worthy of the calling we have received."*

Each of these people have bought voice to these pages, and value to my life. Original thought? Perhaps a little. But more importantly this work before you is the result of a life-long wrestle of the people of God in community with one another who have sought to pursue the heart of our Father at all cost. And as they continue to accept His invitation to deeper encounters of intimacy and love, they are unceasing in their attempts to bring others with them to encounter Him too.

Mark Appleyard
December 2016

Foreword

You are probably reading this book because you are in business, or thinking about starting one. If so, then you live in the "real world" where you have to make practical decisions, manage people and drive real, measurable outcomes. But of all the business books out there, you probably picked up this one because you also hunger to see heaven invade more of your family, business and life. You know that you have access to all of God's wisdom, insight, love and grace which you, as a leader, can pour into your home and business in a way that will call out the best in the people around you and enrich your life in all the ways that really matter. If that is you, then you are definitely reading the right book.

In "Think, Speak, Live, Business from Heaven's Perspective", Pastor Mark Appleyard sets out the Biblical basis for seeing business as Kingdom work. Some have said that we should treat "business as mission". But this book makes it clear that business *is* mission. Why? Because people in business are on the front lines of the world, interacting with all layers of society from retail customers to those in positions of great influence. They have access to and interaction with people that missionaries cannot reach. Because 98% of the people who attend Church will not be in full time church ministry, and many will be in business, church leadership has the duty to equip business leaders to live out their faith and extend the Kingdom in their business spheres. How do we, as business leaders do that?

We need to think like heaven. Transformation comes from the renewing of our minds. Part of that is keeping our eyes fixed on Jesus and ridding ourselves of the "stinkin' thinkin'" that so easily entangles us. Another part is by ensuring that we have our identity firmly rooted in the Father and His love for us, rather than success, security or what others think of us.

We also need to speak like heaven speaks. But like a child, we need to hear properly before we can speak properly. Mark does a wonderful job illustrating what it looks like to tune in and hear from the Father. He then provides practical help on learning to speak a heavenly language, but also to speak truth and life to those around us, manifesting not just the gifts, but the fruit of the Spirit in our lives.

Finally we need to live like heaven. As we press deeper into the Father's heart we will begin to experience greater measures of the abundant life Jesus came to make possible for us. As we seek Him first, we will see fruit in our lives, relationships and indeed businesses as well.

I am excited for you to read this book as I believe it is a jewel box filled with nuggets of treasure. The wisdom and insight in these pages come from Mark's lifetime of service, ministry and business. He is a pastor, an intellectual, an entrepreneur and author. He is an amazing husband and father with a family that reflects the light of heaven they welcome into their home. But Mark is also a former electrician. And that is important. Electricians have to make things work. When the switch is flipped, the light has to come on. So the profound Biblical truths in this book are presented in an earthy, accessible, practical way that business people especially will appreciate. And like electricity or gravity, all of God's truth just seems to work.

My prayer is that you enjoy this book and experience new dimensions of connection with the Father, blessings on your family and business and a life of thinking, speaking and living like heaven.

Mark Stoleson
December 2016

part one

Think Like Heaven

A New Perspective

While it may have been 10 years in the planning, my wife Julie and I finally experienced the thrill of a wedding anniversary in Paris. Ah . . . the city of love. Long walks along the Seine, late night dining in sidewalk cafés and, of course, the customary trip to the top of the Eiffel Tower.

As we stood at the base of Gustav Eiffel's iconic structure with eyes focused upon the viewing platform 984 feet above us, it was only right that, as a chivalrous husband, I asked my wife if she had any concerns regarding her potential for vertigo.

"If we take it slow, I will be fine," was Julie's reply.

Escorting her to the entrance, I paid for our admission, and we began the ascent. First it was the stairs. Many, many stairs. Stairs with a wall of wire mesh rising alongside them, providing the climber with a clear view of just how high he or she was rising with each step. As we progressed, Julie seemed to be gaining a good rhythm to her climb. I seemed to be gaining a good grip on the rail. The higher we went, the tighter I gripped. I kept asking how she was doing, secretly hoping she would say that vertigo was kicking in and that we needed to stop at the lower level. But, no. Julie seemed to gain confidence with every step she climbed.

"Look, honey, you can see all the way to Montmartre!" she said excitedly.

"Is that a fact?" I replied, with my eyes looking nowhere except to the next upward step in front of me.

Once we reached the lower level viewing platform, I mentioned to her that it was beginning to get late and that I would fully understand if she was happy enough to only go this far.

"Oh, no. We have come all this way and paid our money. I want to go *all the way* to the top."

To the elevator we went.

I often wondered how Charlie felt in Willie Wonka's glass elevator as he shot through the roof of the chocolate factory. I don't ponder that sensation anymore.

I could feel the vertigo, like a dark fog, taking over my soul as we rose to the very top. When the glass elevator finally came to a standstill, Julie exited quite hurriedly to the edge of the enclosed viewing area, but my feet felt frozen to the floor. *Surely this is far enough!* I thought. But she wasn't satisfied to stay there; she had to go to the *very* top—the outside top. The top near the antennas that makes a person experience an impending sense of being drawn to the perilous edge and of falling off. Clearly at this point, my ability to project a controlled exterior had faded as I was more concerned about survival than bravado. Julie turned from the edge of the unobstructed view back toward me, and, seeing my obvious distress, reached out her hand and said, "Trust me. It is all good. It is amazing up here."

I did. She was right.

By making the decision to take Julie's hand that day I accepted an invitation to a new perspective. We had been elevated to a higher level, a new position that changed what we saw and how we saw it.

With over twenty years of leadership and pastoral ministry experience, I have observed people who choose to stay positioned at lower levels of their spiritual growth, never accessing the heights of their potential. The lower spiritual growth level is earth—living from the position of earth's perspective. The viewpoint from earth restricts our spiritual growth to our own understanding and experience. It is only possible to see a short spiritual distance from that locale. There are many reasons why people limit their spiritual growth by staying at a level where they only choose to see things from earth's perspective. For some, the reason is fear of the unknown. For others, it is because they don't know how to live any other way. And others still, don't move beyond this position because they believe they don't have access to the kinds of spiritual encounters which others experience.

I am familiar with that lower level, because I chose to position myself there for years, too. I have also worked with many business leaders across the world who remained at this place for years, striving to fulfill their calling to serve Jesus in the marketplace, from a vantage point that was not allowing them to fully do so.

I managed to make a shift. I learned some things—helpful things that made it possible for me to break through what held me at the level of only seeing things from earth's perspective. Breaking through to a higher spiritual realm and seeing from a new point of view, birthed in me a desire to help *you*. I want to help you take in the spiritual view from an elevated level. There is a position at this elevated level that is rightfully yours, because it is a position paid for by Jesus. What I have provided in the pages that follow is a step-by-step guide that will change the spiritual level from which you live. It will elevate your spiritual outlook, so that you can experience the fullness of your spiritual potential and the fullness of God's spiritual power working through you.

The elevated level is heaven. You can live *from* heaven to earth. You can live from there today—now. Imagine living and leading from the level of a new position where your new outlook enables you to have direct access to the conversations of heaven, reveals how you can release the language of heaven, and provides resources enabling you to live as in heaven on the earth. Imagine the implications living and leading this way could have on your relationship with God and with your family and friends, and the consequences for your business relationships. If you take hold of this new elevated position, if you live from the perspective of heaven to earth, thinking, speaking and living like heaven, you will become one of the most influential spiritual leaders in the world. God designed it that way.

So on the pages that follow you will find three sections: Think. Speak. Live. I will demonstrate how you can think how heaven thinks, speak how heaven speaks and live how heaven lives.

I now offer you an invitation. An invitation to access a new spiritual level. A new position that reveals a new perspective. There may be times while reading this book that you encounter a new thought that causes you to experience spiritual vertigo. I ask you, in those moments, to reach out and take my hand through the words on these pages and explore the view I will share.

"Trust me. It is all good. It is amazing up here."

The first step we will take together is learning to listen . . .

I

Can You Hear Me Now?

"Christ opened the understanding of His disciples, and He will open up our understanding and our hearts and will show us wonderful things that we should never know but for the mighty revelation and enlightenment of the Spirit that He gives to us."

—*Smith Wigglesworth*

Can You Hear Me?

"Gary! Do you trust me more than you trust Bill?" I asked with intense sincerity. "Gary, can you hear me? Can you hear me now? How about now? Gary! Are you there?"

Then, thankfully, I heard Gary's relieved voice cut through the static white noise. I also heard frustration. "Yes, that's a Roger. I can hear you!" came his reply. And I understood both his relief and frustration. Nothing about this job was as advertised. We certainly weren't experiencing the clean, safe work environments we'd all seen in the safety videos we had been forced to watch six months earlier.

It was 7:30 AM and the sun was already searing; the summer heat of tropical North Queensland was already strong enough to cause sweaty hands and wringing wet shirts. Gary was hanging ten stories up, off the side of a rusted industrial building. He was harnessed to a single old rope. The sweat mixed with the red dust from the nickel ore of the refinery's production line, along with the height, added to the perils of what was an already dangerous job. And the penetrating putrid smell of raw ammonia, which somehow always found a way to sneak past the seals of the canister masks we were each wearing, made for a miserable way to spend a Tuesday morning.

"Gary, the orange and the gray wires go together, and the bright blue and pink wires *must not* touch each other! Gary, do you copy?!" I barked at him again through the two-way radio while I stared at the crumpled schematic drawings that were way too big to fully stretch out in the temporary office we had made in the truck.

"What do you mean, not the blue and pink wires? Bill told us just the opposite. He insisted that the orange and gray ones MUST NOT touch!" Bill was a co-worker, a good guy, but he was wrong, mortally wrong.

"Gary, I promise you, mate, if you touch the blue and pink wires together, you will not only blow up the motor's variable speed drive, you will also light yourself up like a Christmas tree!" There was a pause, "Gary, can you hear me?"

"What? Of course, I can hear you!"

"Do you trust me?"

"What a stupid thing to say. Of course I do."

Then I asked again, "Do you trust me more than you trust Bill?"

"Yes, more than Bill." There was a pause. "I see how you are at work."

Gary's response surprised me. "What do you mean?" I asked.

"I see you at the beginning of each day in the corner behind the work shed, where you think no one can see you, praying. I see you spending time with Jim and Peter, blokes nobody wants to bother with. You are always encouraging them and helping them to be better people. And I am guessing that when you pray behind the work shed, you pray for everyone's safety. Given the insane and crazy things we all have to do out here, and the fact that we are all still alive, it tells me you know something, someone, the rest of us don't. So yeah. . . I trust you—the orange and gray wires it is!"

Silence.

Then came the quiet, low, dull, whirring sound we had both been waiting to hear, as the motor slowly came back online. "I'm glad I trusted you more than bloody Bill," crackled Gary. "Looks like another win for the big bloke upstairs!"

A Familiar Voice?

"Can you hear me?" "Can you hear me now?" "How about now?"

Years ago I was invited to lead a time of devotion for a large Christian company based in Charlotte, North Carolina. Given that marketplace ministry is near and dear to my heart and one in which I have experience, I was specifically asked to teach on the role of the executive leader in expanding the Kingdom of heaven on earth.

Positioned around the large oak boardroom table were ten executives on four-wheeled *rolly* office chairs. Each individual functioned at different levels within the organization. I had an idea about how to open my presentation, by telling them a story about red dust and how one time I had a co-worker friend named Gary.

Then I began to teach. It went something like this . . . .

How often does God speak to us throughout the course of any given day, how often does heaven seek to get our attention? The static, the white noise of deadlines, reports, board meetings and the endless list of stress-inducing things, these distractions interfere with our spiritual auditory senses to the point we become dulled to the sound of the voice that is seeking to penetrate through--the voice of our heavenly Father who is always speaking to us.

After accepting the atonement of Jesus Christ for our sins, we begin the process of spiritual transformation. We experience a new alive and gain access to a new place because of a new position. The *new* alive is a regenerated spirit; the *new* place is heaven; our *new* position is that of a son or daughter. Jesus revealed how to live life from the new place and new position, and gave us a mandate to live the same way He did, *"On earth as it is in heaven."* He showed us how to hear and see from heaven, He revealed how to live from heaven to earth. He was the perfect example of what it means to live confidently as the child of a loving, always-good heavenly Father.

Both our positional identity and our spiritual identity shift when we say yes to Jesus. We suddenly gain spiritual body parts we didn't possess before. When we become sons and daughters of a loving heavenly Father we are given "New Ears," "Big Ears," "Spiritual Ears," "Heaven's Ears . . . ."

"Heaven's Ears" are part of the new alive that comes with our new position as sons or daughters of the Kingdom of heaven.

Living *from* the Kingdom of heaven in the marketplace in tangible ways assumes an ability to hear and listen. If we don't know how to hear and listen from heaven, we don't know how to think new thoughts, heaven's thoughts. We have been invited to discard old thought patterns and learn to think like heaven thinks.

For the first fifteen minutes I shared with the executive leaders how we have been invited to think and live from heaven to earth; how we have been invited to hear from heaven in every area of our lives, including business. Everything was going swimmingly. I spoke with passion and authority. We were having fun. Board members nodded at the right time. They enjoyed the story of the red dust and how my faith walk had influenced Gary. They laughed at my jokes, especially the one about the emu with the long legs who agrees with everything the man at the bar says, and they were postured in such a way as to grant me permission to continue, except for one fella.

At the sixteen-minute mark, just after I had just addressed how we, as children of God, must learn how to listen and hear from heaven in every area of our lives, the meeting took an unexpected turn.

One of the board members, let's call him Chris, because I like Chris as a name, began to get agitated. He started swiveling and knocking his chair arms forcibly against the big oak table, hard enough to spill some of the less thirsty board members' glasses of water.

Then at the seventeen-minute mark, in one giant thrust of his arms against the table, Chris pushed his rolly chair backwards spilling even more water from full glasses. Then, with several well-placed expletives, he informed me that he found my teaching to be quite disagreeable.

"This is a waste of my time. I've never heard God speak!" he said. And somewhere in the distance, a dog barked.

The atmosphere in the room became instantly tense. Looking across the oak boardroom table, I observed two very different things happening.

First, there was the incidental activity of the nine non-eye-contacting executives who were trying their hardest to become invisible. Some were attempting to wipe the water on the table away, left to right, right to left. Others seemed to have suddenly found the pattern of the carpet to be quite fascinating.

Then there was the tense faced, rolly-chair-thrusting, Chris, whose angry gaze I meet with calm thankfulness. I was grateful for Chris' outburst; I wasn't there to stroke egos or to give pretty words. Because of Chris, I could cut to the chase. He had unknowingly forced us to address the real question every Christian high-level executive leader wants answered.

The question goes something like this: "*I know God exists. I know He is head of His church. I know I am part of His existing church. However, I don't know how my business or I fit in to His master plan. And what's more, I don't know how to know, because I am not convinced I even know when speaks to me.*"

"Chris, you seem pretty angry. I'm guessing you didn't suddenly arrive at your opinion while sitting here. Would you please expound?"

Chris began to spill, among other things, that he was living with a girl whom he had managed to get pregnant. He wasn't sure he wanted to continue in the relationship, let alone be a father. Given the context of his immediate situation, he didn't feel that God had any interest in speaking to him, or anyone else for that matter. He had tried many years before to read the Bible, but he found its message irrelevant. Heaven, in his technicolor outburst, had no voice in the world today.

There it was! A hinge on which this seemingly impossible impasse could swing, an opportunity to throw open the door and fill the room with Kingdom life. You see, a person can only provide answers to people with questions. Chris had exposed the real question.

"Allow me to build a hypothetical" I said.

Chris nodded.

"Let's all assume for one moment that you and the girl you are currently living with met for the first time six months ago. And let's continue to build the hypothetical by suggesting that apart from an initial conversation of thirty minutes when you first met, you have not spoken to her since that day to now."

Chris nodded and the remaining nine fellas looked quizzical but also intrigued. This was real life, and they all knew it.

"Let's also suggest that rather than have all eleven of us sitting around our oak board table today, that we are in fact standing around enjoying some refreshments and nibbles, having a grand old time, talking about all manner of trivial things.

While we are in this state of muted office revelry, with our backs turned toward the door, who should walk in, giggling and laughing with her friends? None other, than the girl you met six months before, had a half hour conversation with, but have not spoken to since—are we clear?"

An attentive, "Yes," came from Chris.

"Now, Chris, would you know who it was that had just walked through the door, given your back was turned?"

"No," came his truthful reply.

"Now," I said, "Let's go back to that first encounter and build a second hypothetical. Let's say you met her six months ago, had an initial conversation with her for thirty minutes, but then, instead of not talking to her again, you began to speak with her for thirty minutes each day over the following six months leading up to today. Here we are, office revelry, drinks, nibbles, backs to the door, your girl walks in laughing and giggling with her friends, would you know who it was that just walked in the room?"

"Yes, of course I would," Chris responded somewhat irritably.

"The ten-million-dollar question, Chris, is, `Why?' Why would you know who it was in the second hypothetical?"

With his head beginning to nod, his rolly chair returning to its proper resting place, he replied, "Because I know what she sounds like. Her voice would be familiar."

"Now, we are getting somewhere!" I said.

Quietly, but directly, I went on. "Chris, it is clear to me that you haven't ever really spent sustained quality time with God. You might have prayed a prayer or two in your life, even spent a lot of time in church hearing others pray, but you haven't ever spent sustained time with Him *yourself*. But Chris, believe me when I say this—He has been passionately speaking to you all these years, you just don't know the sound of His voice in the room. You don't know how to hear and listen."

Then, with the full attention of everyone in the room I asked Chris a question I hope to answer in this book.

"Chris, would you like to hear Him? Would you be interested in me giving you four letters that, if applied for sustained periods of time, will give you the ability to hear what heaven says, so that you can think how heaven thinks?"

Before Chris could respond, one of the board members piped up, "I want to know!" Not to be left out, the remaining eight fellas chimed in as well. They, too, sought this knowledge.

And so did Chris.

Four Letters to Hear Heaven

Pastor Wayne is one of my mentors. He founded a church in the late 1990s in Hawaii called *New Hope*. Pastor Wayne and New Hope Church have been instrumental in training up pastors around the world, including me. Thirteen years ago Pastor Wayne visited Melbourne, where we lived at the time. He gave a message that changed my life. In his message were four letters, spiritual tools that, when applied through journaling, gave me the ability to hear what heaven says. Pastor Wayne described it as *"Life Journaling."*

I have given these same four spiritual tools to thousands of people over the years since. I have discovered that these four letters, if applied for sustained periods of time through journaling, will give sons and daughters the ability to eavesdrop in on the conversations of heaven and learn to think how heaven thinks. These four letters, if applied for sustained periods of time, give us a capacity to shepherd ourselves, shepherd our families, and shepherd our businesses and staff in ways we have never even dreamed possible.

I have seen many people develop the ability to tune into the sounds of heaven and begin to think how heaven thinks because of these four letters. The four letters are S, O, A, and P.

That's right, SOAP! And it is right that the acronym spells out SOAP because this practice leads us to the One who cleans us from the inside out. As an executive leader, you know that nothing about the job is as advertised. The decisions you must make daily aren't made in "clean, safe work environments." Often you are faced with deals that seek to undermine your integrity. You are faced with conflict and tough decisions in which you want to hear God and know how heaven thinks.

SOAP tunes our hearts back to the sounds of His voice and brings realignment to our identity.

SOAP stands for: Scripture. Observation. Application. Prayer.

Journaling using the SOAP method is a highly interactive process of practicing how to experience God's presence. It is about practicing to hear God during an intentional quiet time, so we can become good at hearing Him in the midst of the pressures of our day. As Pastor Wayne shared with me and as I have learned from experience, we can learn to hear and understand the inflections and tones of His voice. We can grow familiar with how heaven sounds.

We can learn the kinds of things that He says and how He says them to such a point that we can be in a hostile meeting, or a conflict at home, or struggling to know what direction to take our business, and suddenly we have peace and joy because we hear Him!

In the midst of the static white noise of distracting thoughts or in the hurtful conflict of words, with our spiritual back turned toward the door, we can hear a sound and know that we know that God just showed up and He is speaking. How? Because we have spent time with Him every day, because we know Him by the sound of His voice, we have grown familiar.

How to Journal

Before I go any further, you have to know that SOAP requires us to exercise faith--faith that God is good, faith that He is always speaking to us, and faith that we can hear Him. Jesus taught us in Matthew 7:7 to ask, seek and knock, and He promised that when we ask, *"it will be given to [us],"* when we seek, *"[we] will find,"* and when we knock, *"the door will be opened to [us]"* (NIV).

The fact is, God wants us to hear and listen to Him more than we want to hear and listen to Him. He desires to converse with us, and He is passionate that we would know *"the mystery of His will according to His good pleasure, which He purposed in Christ..."* (Ephesians 1:9). He wants to reveal how heaven thinks so we can know and live from heaven to earth!

So let's get started. . . .

First you will need your Bible, a notebook, and a pen. Find a Bible reading plan online—www.biblegateway.com has some good Bible reading plan options. It doesn't matter which plan you use, just use one.

Keep the first five or six pages in your notebook blank because you are going to need them soon.

For the purpose of coaching you, let's choose the book of Acts, and we will start in Chapter four.

As you prepare to read, pray a simple prayer. I usually pray something like, "Holy Spirit, you are here today to lead me into all truth. I ask that as I read the truth of your Word today, You will highlight to me the things I need to know. I pray that You would mentor me in the ways of the Kingdom. In Jesus' name. Amen."

Take the time to read and listen. Do not rush. Read and listen for heaven's voice.

At some point there is going to be a Scripture verse, or even just a word that will jump out at you as you read. In all the years of journaling, I have only known one or two times where this didn't happen. Remember, you asked God to speak to you. You are seeking and He wants to be found. On those very rare occasions where nothing seemed to jump out at me, I have gone back to a favorite Scripture and journaled again from there.

At this point stop and underline the passage or word that has jumped out, because this is the Scripture God wants to speak to you about today. If it seems totally irrelevant to your current set of circumstances, don't be concerned, it just means He is preparing and equipping you for something down the track—He's just that good!

You now have another opportunity to learn the art of listening to His voice, to hear from heaven. Ask Him if He wants you to pause your reading at the highlighted Scripture, or if you are to continue on. Even if it is the opening sentence, go through this exercise. Once you have your answer, simply obey.

When your reading time is done, take the Scripture you have been given and, leaving the top line of your page blank, write it out in full in your notebook. If you have been given half a chapter, then look at condensing it down. Typically, you will be given one to three verses.

Having done this exercise, I stopped at verses 32-35, and wrote them out accordingly. Below I work through the process of SOAP.

S (Scripture): "All the believers were united in heart and mind. And they felt that what they owned was not their own, so they shared everything they had. The apostles testified powerfully to the resurrection of the Lord Jesus, and God's great blessing was upon them all. There were no needy people among them, because those who owned land or houses would sell them and bring the money to the apostles to give to those in need." (Acts 4:32-35).

Having written the Scripture down, you now have your "S."

The next two steps will require you asking a couple of questions. The "O" question goes something like this: *"What is this Scripture saying about itself?"* The goal of *observation* is to put the Scripture you have been given into your own words, and keep your paraphrase to a paragraph if you can. Keeping things succinct is important, because doing so causes you to get specific with what God is saying. For Acts 4:32-35, I wrote the following:

O (observation): *"Kingdom perspective changes the way people see things. It changes the way we see each other. One person's opinion is no more or less important when united around the message of Kingdom. One person's resources are not more important than another's when united around the message of the Kingdom. No one person's needs are less important than others when united around the message of the Kingdom. This perspective is fully-fledged Kingdom culture in action."*

Having written down your succinct observation, you are now ready to ask another question. This question is the laser pointer onto your heart that Holy Spirit wants to impress on you. The question is, "How is my life going to be different today, on the basis of the Scripture I have been given and the observation I have made?" The application should have "I" statements and "me" statements. After all, God is speaking to you about how He sees you, not how He sees your church, your spouse, your kids, your business or even the neighbor who ran his keys down the side of your car because you parked in his space again!

Back to Acts 4:32-35, here is what I wrote for *application*.

> A (application): *"The key for me to live in Kingdom community is the message of the Kingdom, not my opinions, the supply of my resources, or even the function of my ministry. These all flow out from the message. The more I allow the message of the Kingdom to flow out from me, the more alignment my lifestyle and attitudes towards others will be affected. The message that God loves me, that I am a person of divine royalty, that I am a son of heaven, a co-heir with Christ, needs to fill my heart and mind every waking moment."*

The "P" is for a *prayer of appropriation*. It is your time to simply come before God and acknowledge you have heard His voice and with His help, are going to do something about it today.

It may sound something like this:

> P (prayer): *"Father, thank You for the message of the Kingdom. Help me to believe the truth over my life that flows out from this astonishingly good news. In Jesus' matchless name. Amen."*

We are almost there. The most important part is what follows, because it is the part that unlocks this message to you continually throughout the course of any given day. That part is the "Title". Read back over your new journal entry and ask Holy Spirit to give you a title for what He has just revealed to you.

I titled Acts 4:32-35, "Living From A Promoted Perspective." That may even come up later in this book—who knew?

On the top of your completed entry, place the Scripture reference and a page number. Given this is your first entry, this page will obviously be number one.

Last, go to the front of your journal and draw up a "Table Of Contents." This will help you keep a chronicled daily, monthly yearly account of where God has led you. Over time your table of contents will reveal to you how your future always makes sense in light of the past.

The table of contents is simple; just one line that shows your Scripture reference, your title and the page number.

Congratulations on completing your first journal entry.

Think Like Heaven Thinks

Several years ago I was in a meeting that was not fruitful or productive in any way. Tensions were high and resolution seemed like an impossibility. I know, I am the first person in world history to have that experience. . . .

I was leading the meeting, and each time we thought we were getting somewhere, we hit yet another roadblock. The sound of my team's raised voices was beginning to mash together in my mind. It sounded more like static white noise.

Gary, can you hear me. . . .

In the midst of the statements, suddenly clarity came. It came in the form of a picture in my mind. Immediately, some words accompanied the picture. Although they felt familiar, they seemed different to any words I would typically say in a moment like the one I found myself in. But because of my years of intentional journaling, because I had practiced listening to God through SOAP, because I had grown familiar with what heaven sounds like, because I was learning how to think like heaven thinks, I recognized God's voice.

I gestured with my hands for everyone to quiet down. I walked over to the white board, drew the picture I was given, and the words that accompanied it, then sat down. There was complete silence in the room as the weight of what I had placed on the board sank in. The picture that God gave me provided the very direction we needed in order to make our way forward as a team.

On my way out the door that night, a team member stopped me to make an observation about the events, particularly what had happened with the white board. He said, "When you got up and started drawing I thought you were having a moment of disconnection with reality. Given what was going on in the room, it seemed irrelevant and a little crazy. But by the time you sat back down, the atmosphere had changed. We all knew we had heard from heaven. And I found myself wondering, "What book did he get this from? It's gold!" And then it dawned on me. You didn't get this from any book. You only get this kind of stuff from sitting at Jesus' feet."

"Gary, do you trust me more than you trust Bill?"

The fact is, in life and leadership, nothing about this job is as advertised. We must become familiar with His voice, we must hear from heaven!

God wants us to know His voice above all other voices, even the "Bills" in your life. He is on the other end saying, "Can you hear me? Can you hear me now?" And what He wants to tell us is of infinite importance. It's the truth that sets us free, the wisdom of eternity, the peace that surpasses understanding, the joy that becomes our strength, the light that guides our path, and the rock that makes our feet firm.

As we continue together through the pages that follow, I invite you to tune in your "New Ears," "Big Ears," "Spiritual Ears." Your heavenly Father is calling to you. He has something to say. He wants you to hear from heaven and think like heaven thinks.

So there was a man who walked into a bar and saw another man sitting at the bar next to an emu with very long legs...

2

Position and Potential

"To the degree that we embrace the truth that our identity is not rooted in our success, power, or popularity, but in God's infinite love, to that degree can we let go of our need to judge."

—*Henry J.M. Nouwen*

Toy World

"I grew up in a small three-bedroom cottage nestled between the green rolling hills of dairy farming country in South Gippsland, Australia. It was remote; the nearest town may as well have been on the moon. I was the youngest of seven children, three girls and four boys. Born in the 1970s but raised in the 1940s, our home was so small that our one bathroom was located in the garden. The water heater was fire powered and had to be lit by us boys early in the morning if the girls were to have a warm bath. Rooms were shared, beds were shared, clothing, even baths, all shared. Those were the humble beginnings in which we built our lives, developed our dreams and became excruciatingly familiar with each other, and with our loving parents.

While I am sure all of my older siblings would disagree, it was *hard* being the youngest.

The youngest watches everybody else get to do all the cool stuff;

the youngest has to stay home while everyone else has adventures. And when the youngest does get to go out, he has to wear hand me down pajama's in public!

Every youngest child knows all the best things happen *after* they have been sent to bed or have to go home with their parents.

When I was five, I got the rare and exciting opportunity to ride with my Dad to a neighboring town to do some grocery shopping – just the two of us! To me, this rural town of 2500 people was the equivalent of a Vegas trip today with all the shiny lights, buildings, and people. The grocery store had electric pony rides for five cents a turn and candy displays that seemed endless.

After picking out groceries, and yielding to my canny tactics to gain a piece of candy from the epic candy displays, my Dad did the only thing a respectable father would do, he took his very well behaved son to Toy World. Toy World was just a short walk from the grocery store, and it was the mecca for any boy or girl of five!

Even after all these years, I can still feel the rise in my spirits when, standing at the front door, he let go of my hand and said, "Wander around for a while Mark. I'll wait over there." I imagine he pointed to somewhere specific, but I was already on the move. Finally, someone with some sense! I was free, released to take browsing matters into my own hands, to finally have my own adventure—and I wasn't even wearing pajama's!

Having been released from the grip of my Dad's hand, I headed straight down the never-ending isle of Lego, Lego of every kind; space Lego, farm Lego, fireman and police Lego, Lego that lit up, Lego that rolled, even Lego boats. I was in Lego heaven.

Then I turned the corner to see bicycles, then another corner—kites. Then another, and then another until I turned around and realized I had no idea how to get back to Dad. I probably should have paid more attention to where he'd pointed.

I was lost. Suddenly this wasn't Lego heaven, this was that other place.

I began to panic and because I grew up in farm country, I also began *mooing*. You know, the loud somewhat annoying sound a cow makes to get the attention of the farmer when they are stuck, want something, are in pain, or in my situation, lost. It wasn't a literal mooing, but you get the idea.

Unfortunately, my father couldn't hear me over the 5 million other little boys and girls perusing the suddenly hellish land of glitter and plenty. I wandered. I yelled. I cried. I mooed, he didn't answer.

What happened next is something I think we can all relate to. While the truth is that I had wandered off and was lost, it felt like something far more devastating; it felt like my Dad had abandoned me.

"What if he had left me to forever wander the endless isles of Toy World alone?" That thought took hold and began to haunt my little heart.

Looking back, the one emotion that stands out above all others is the great sense of insecurity. I was still Mark Appleyard, the youngest child of a large family that lived in very close proximity and loved each other well. But knowing who *I* was didn't make me secure. It never does.

Because of my Dad's *seeming* abandonment, I suddenly felt terribly insecure and what's more, I *seemed* to have lost all security and access to my identity.

It's an odd thing to lose a sense of security and identity simply because you get lost in the glitter and plenty of a toy store. But I was only five. And I would like to suggest that my five-year-old identity and security couldn't support the freedom and power my Dad had given me to navigate Toy World on my own. I wasn't firmly positioned yet... but I'll get to that later.

There are two things I want to highlight from this story right now. The first, our heavenly Father is always good and He will never leave nor forsake us. It is not in His nature. It is paramount that we make this the foundation of our faith – that our heavenly Father loves us and He will *never* leave nor forsake us. And the second is to *never* wander Toy

World alone – never!

With that foundation set, I want to spend the lion share of this chapter focusing on the first point: regardless of our circumstances, who we are doesn't change. We are sons and daughters of an always good, loving Father, and we must learn how to live secure in our identity if we are to walk out the purposes of God in our lives, if we are to walk in freedom and power.

One of the signs we truly know who we are is that we truly know that our heavenly Father is always near. If we truly know who we are, we won't entertain the feelings of abandonment that seek to destroy us because we know leaving is never an option for Him. If we confidently know who we are, surely we also know heavenly Father's nature and character; that he is an always-good Father, and we are indeed his beloved...

A False Sense of Security

Brian was a successful businessman in charge of a large and growing company. He had quickly risen to gargantuan success in his field of choice. His was the usual rags to riches story; hard work, grit, right place at the right time. Sprinkle that with gutsy decisions most people wouldn't make and, voilà!

From an outside glance, Brian was living the dream; trophy wife, gorgeous well-mannered kids who were doing great in school, best boat, best car, best friends, best teeth, biggest house – a likeable guy in a healthy growing church that had placed him on their finance committee, of course. What was not to like?

It came as a complete shock at first, when on the local current affairs show, I saw the investigative reporters storming his offices; his staff running like a plague of mice when a cat enters the room. The next scene was Brian behind his desk, phone in hand, bright lights, his left hand pushing the camera lens away from his perplexed face and perfect teeth. What was this? What could have happened to Brian?

Several months later, through a pastor friend of mine who was close to Brian, I came to discover that he had taken several unsound risks, a few ethically questionable *short-cuts*, and wasn't able to deliver on promises to his clients. In short, he had believed his own press about always making the right decisions.

Digging deeper, I learned Brian had actually climbed higher than his identity and his security could sustain. He had gotten lost in Lego hell. Brian had been propelled through the ceiling of success only to discover the floor of his identity couldn't support him standing at the new height. We have all seen it. Perhaps it has been you. Perhaps it currently *is* you.

The following months of despair and turmoil in his business, personal and spiritual life, became evidence of this reality. He suddenly found himself standing exposed and insecure in the land of glitter and plenty wondering why his heavenly Father had abandoned him. The mooing was loud and public, but it wasn't helping him find the security he was looking for, the security he was designed for.

Grown, educated, successful, reasonable believing adults are consistently held back from being all God has called them to be because of an inaccurate understanding of their heavenly Father and therefore their identity. This leads to feelings of insecurity. Eventually we will turn a corner and feel abandoned and insecure. We will find ourselves wandering around in a hellish land of glitter and plenty.

It is one thing to feel abandoned by an earthly authority figure, but to feel abandoned by God is something totally different. It is a game changer. Many of you know this to be true.

King David felt it when being chased by Saul in the mountains, as recorded in Psalm 13,

> "O Lord, how long will you forget me? Forever? How long will you look the other way? How long must I struggle with anguish in my soul,

with sorrow in my heart every day?"

Perhaps you haven't turned around enough corners to feel this way yet. Perhaps you are still enamored by all the shiny things that can steal your attention from where your dad pointed he would be waiting for you: new cars, new homes, great press, new relationships, new promotion, new investment opportunity, Legos of every shape and size... But I guarantee, if you aren't living secure regarding your identity in Christ; you are building your house on the sand.

For Brian, his false understanding of his own identity was that God would only be pleased with him if he performed successfully. He felt he was only deserving of conditional love. As though his dad might abandon him in Toy World if he didn't live up to expectations. It is highly probable that his primary authority figure growing up only showed affection and approval when he performed well. Whatever the root cause, his lack of understanding regarding who he was in God led to his insecurity. Sadly, his success provided a false sense of security and only reinforced a false identity.

Because of his need to feel secure, he had no option but to do what you or I would do if we measured our security the same way; he kept taking the next big risk, even the ethically questionable risk, in order to keep the same results flowing, to ensure a sense of emotional security between himself and his heavenly Father.

Brian needed to know who his heavenly Father truly was: that He was good, He hadn't left Brian to wander in Toy World alone, that Brian's security wasn't connected to his performance, and that he was a beloved son.

What if Brian *could* know his true identity as a child of an always-good Father? How would that affect the seeming absence of His presence? I imagine he would wander the isles more patiently, knowing full-well that his heavenly Father was there and would take his hand again. I believe he would understand that, in fact, he is never truly out of his heavenly Father's care. He would gain a promotion in his perspective.

Who Are You?

Who are you? Can you fully answer that question beyond a shadow of a doubt? Do you know your true identity?

I'm not writing about the nauseating Christian culture cliché answer to this question – the one that fades away at the slightest hiccup. I am writing about the kind of answer that the likes of John Wesley had when standing in the face of his deadly foe at Bolton – he kept preaching, because he was not afraid to die.

Or perhaps like Charles Finney, who refused to come down from the hill behind his house until he had a life-altering encounter with God. Then there was Smith Wigglesworth; so solid in his identity that he would rebuke death in the face of anger and ridicule. Or Maria Woodworth Etter, who after the death of five of her children and her own near death, stood as a woman in a man's world and went on to preach to hundreds of thousands of people—some of the hardest known hellions of her day.

These were all world changers, children of God secure in their identity and living as expressions of His Kingdom come. They revealed what it looks like when a son or daughter lives secure. They navigated Toy World with confidence and purpose!

So, I ask again. Do you really know who you are and what your purpose is before God? Are you so sure of your identity in your heavenly Father that when things in your world go falteringly wrong, you remain secure in your identity? Or, when things go awry, are you one of the many who are mooing in the isles, feeling abandoned by Him?

Consider this, once we say *yes* to Jesus, once we experience our new alive, three things happen to us that alter our old identity and give us access to a promoted perspective. These three things are: we have a new *position*, a new *potential*, and access to a new *power*. In the remainder of this chapter I want to explore our new position and new potential. I have committed the entire next chapter to our new power.

Our New Potential

"...For you are a chosen people. You are royal priests, a holy nation, God's very own possession. As a result, you can show others the goodness of God, for he called you out of the darkness into his wonderful light." (1 Peter 2:9).

Because of original sin, humanity was lost. All mankind was mooing in Toy World. Then, in Exodus 19:5-6, God gave the nation of Israel the promise of a new position. They were to become, in their new position, a kingdom of priests, a holy nation under God. He would not abandon us!

This new position was a forerunner of things to come. It was based firmly upon the Abrahamic Covenant as seen in the Old Testament's version of the "Great Commission" found in Genesis 12:3,

"...all the nations of the earth will be blessed through you."

Priests in the Old Testament were mediators between God and man, servants of a good master. They were positioned closest to arc of the covenant in the temple, the presence of God; and they interceded on behalf of the nation. The priests were in the Levitical line of the twelve tribes of Israel, and were led by one priest in particular, the High Priest. The High Priest would offer sacrifices each year on behalf of the nation for the forgiveness of their sins.

Crossing over into the New Testament, the book of Hebrews reveals that we too have a High Priest. The difference being that He is an eternal High Priest. Jesus, as our eternal High Priest, offered Himself once for all, for the sins of the world. So now, in Christ, our eternal High Priest, we have become *royal* priests, we have a new position. We are no longer simply servants to a good Master, we are royalty, we are in the family; we are sons and daughters to an always-good Father

"For you are all children of God through faith in Christ Jesus." (Galatians 3:26).

And,

"See how very much our Father loves us, for he calls us his children, and that is what we are!" (1 John 3:1).

We have been positioned as sons and daughters to a good Father. We are royal priests. Because of the work and position of Jesus, the writer to the Hebrews has rightfully declared we are invited into the deepest places of intimacy with the Father. Hebrews 4:16 says,

"So let us come boldly to the throne of our gracious God."

While the priests in the Old Testament had close proximity to His presence, it is nothing in comparison to what it means to be a *royal* priest today. A priest in the Old Testament wasn't in a personal, intimate love relationship with God.

References in the Old Testament to God's children, such as Hosea 11:1-2, are primarily a reference to the nation of Israel as a collective relationship, rather than reference to an individual, personal love relationship. New Testament believers are not only referred to as children of God in a collective sense, they are also referred to as children of God on an individual basis.

I want you to stop for one moment and say aloud four times, *"I am heavenly royalty!"* Come on, I said *four* times, *aloud*! Hear yourself declare the truth. Children of the King are nothing less than royal princes and princesses of heaven, sons and daughters of the divine Father. *That* is who you are.

If you have found yourself wandering the Lego isle, you need not be afraid. He has not abandoned you in the world of glittery things. Cast your mooing sounds aside for He has turned our mooing... oops,

I mean, our mourning into dancing, our sorrows into joy!

It's amazing because from the beginning, God has had a mission to bring all people's back into a love relationship with Himself, and He as the High Priest has chosen to use His royal priesthood, those who are relationally positioned in Him to be the *vehicle* for His purposes on earth as it is in heaven.

As royal priests, we have become mediators between God and humanity. Another way of putting it is, we are *mobile temples*...

The Church Has Left the Building

Years ago, I had the chance to visit Thailand. One thing in particular that I loved about that beautiful country was the mobile food cart. From Chang Mai in the north to Bangkok in the south, no matter where we went, there was always someone on a motorbike, a food cart attached to its side filled with hot sticky rice, meat, and vegetables. When we were hungry, there was no need to wait until we got home to eat. We didn't even need to find a restaurant. The food was always there, wherever we were. And it was so good!

Unlike the temple priests in the Old Testament, who turned up for work each day in the same place, we have a *mobile priestly* function. We are a mobile temple. Not a temple of bricks and mortar, but a temple of the heart that reveals the goodness of God to a world desperately in need of Him.

Our mobile priestly function is incarnational and is designed by God to permeate the cracks and crevices of our sphere of influence in society. Our purpose is to live secure as royal priests revealing our High Priest. We are created to live sure in our identity as sons and daughters expressing our Father's goodness on earth as it is in heaven. This doesn't mean that people gain access for the forgiveness of sins through us, but it does mean that when people come in contact with us, they should be able to gain access to the resources of heaven and the tangible presence of our good God working though us.

Back in the first part of this century, I had the opportunity to lead a church through the transitional phase of selling their property. The small church building and piece of land was located in the middle of town abutting a neighboring shopping center and directly opposite the local elementary school. Given the proximity to so many people each day, and knowing that the building would remain intact for at least twelve months, we negotiated into the contract that we wanted to be able to place a sign on the abandoned church building. The very large sign read,

"The Church Has Left the Building!"

Yes, the church has left the building because the temple is now mobile. People don't have to wait for Sunday morning. They don't need to go to a building or an event to access God. They can gain access to Him personally, through those who are living in their new positional love relationship with Him as mobile temples.

As mobile royal priests, we are both a gathered and a scattered community. The royal priestly *position*, is akin to an ambassadorship role that, positionally speaking, gives us full authority to speak on behalf of the Kingdom of God wherever He places us. So, from our new position we have complete authority to join with the Apostle Paul when he says in 2 Corinthians 5:20,

"So we are Christ's ambassadors; God is making his appeal through us. We speak for Christ when we plead, "Come back to God!"

Seated in Heavenly Places

One last thought on our new position. Romans 8:16 tells us that our spirit has joined with His Spirit; and in Ephesians 2:6, we are reminded that our new position is not just relational, it is also a cosmic.

We *"are seated with Him [Christ] in heavenly realms."* Notice the tense is *present.* Therefore, if we are physically here on earth in a geographical location on a given day and time in history, and we, through our connection with His Spirit and unity with Christ are also *currently,* cosmically seated with Christ in heavenly realms, then we are in fact, *positioned* in two places at once. In the Spirit, we are actually both here and there, and because of this we can eavesdrop on the conversations of heaven!

The reality of our new *position* lays the foundation for our new potential. Paul wrote to our Ephesian brothers and sisters the following declaration to leave no doubt concerning the increase in the potential they now possessed as sons and daughters,

"Now all glory to God, who is able, through his mighty power at work within us, to accomplish infinitely more than we might ask or think" (Ephesians 3:20).

Our New Potential

In Matthew 28:19-20, Jesus gave us His Great Commission, *"Go therefore and make disciples of all nations..."*

The Greek word for go is *meta*; it translates as *with, in the midst, behind, between.* Over us, under us, beside us, and definitely before us! Jesus could well have said, "I am all around you." Or "I would never send you into Toy World alone." There is no place where we are that He is not. His go was also His promise that He would be *with* us.

Soon after His commission, Jesus sent Holy Spirit to dwell in us. He had told us in John 14:17 that the Holy Spirit would dwell in us. He used the Greek work *en* meaning, *a fixed position in place, time or state.* Jesus could well have said, "Holy Spirit is stuck inside of you!"

Then there is 1 John 2:20 where Jesus reveals how we are *anointed* by Holy Spirit. This is the Greek word, *charisma* meaning, *to smear*. Each time I read this passage I am reminded of the mischievous look on my childhood friend's face. Richard lived on the farm near to us. He was a lot of fun, mostly because he was a bit of a troublemaker. He particularly loved to prank his siblings. I can still see him positioned just inside the barn doors waiting for his brother's arrival. He held a very large jar of molasses. As Daniel walked into the barn, Richard tipped the entire jar over his head. It went everywhere! Daniel saw me first. He knew I was in on it. When he caught me, he made sure that what was smeared on him was also smeared on me.

My point is, it's impossible to get hugged by a molasses covered boy and not get covered in molasses. John could well have said, "Holy Spirit is all over you, and when you touch people, you're going to leave some of His presence behind."

Our new potential is found as we go in and are smeared with Holy Spirit.

A pastor friend and mentor, Russell Hinds, had a great way of describing the effects of the new potential we get to enjoy when we have a new position. He would often say, "God has given us new eyes to see with, new ears to hear with, and a new strength to live by."

You have access to new *potential* because of a new *position*. Your new potential is all because of God, it is all from God, and it is immeasurable just like God. As Psalms 147:5 puts it,

"How great is our Lord! His power is absolute! His understanding is beyond comprehension!"

Your identity is secured in His infinite understanding and complete power. God has equipped you with the spiritual potential necessary to be who He has created you to become.

Four times. You know the drill, *"I am heavenly royalty, with new potential, equipped by a limitless God."*

Knowledge of who He is informs us about who heaven says we are. He will not abandon us to wander alone in the aisles of life and leadership. He is with us, on us and in us. Knowing who He is informs us about the potential that now rests inside us. He will not place us in aisles where you cannot fulfill His purposes.

Living in the fullness of our new potential is possible due to our new position, but to maximize it will require the activation of another supernatural resource available to us. Get ready to access your new power made available to you.

3

Power and Authority

"The Holy Spirit . . . seemed to go through me, body and soul. I could feel the impression, a wave of electricity, going through and through me. It seemed to come in waves of liquid love."

—Charles Finney

Qualified to Steward the Power

"The opportunity to train with BHP Steel Company as an electrician was an amazing opportunity, and I knew it.

In the 1980s and early 1990s, Australia experienced an economic downturn referred to by then Treasurer, Paul Keeting, as, "the recession we had to have." Jobs were hard to come by and many companies, particularly in the building industry, were folding. Business fundamentals both good and bad were exposed and companies either became more efficient or they died.

BHP was the largest private company in Australia. During these recession years the management of BHP heightened efficiency in its procedures and processes to remain competitive. Because of this fact, they didn't permit young electrical trainees, like myself, to handle important equipment until they were absolutely confident such trainees were fully ready. At the cost of around $1000 per minute, lost production was something they could ill afford.

So the day I was given access to the main electrical switch-room of one of the major production lines, no small permission was granted. It was affirmation; I had been given authority. Those in charge believed I could be trusted with something significant. It was their way of saying, "You are now qualified to steward the power."

Literally. . . .

Our New Power

Jesus displayed a life of power. He walked the planet revealing what it looks like to live as a child of God with full access to how heaven thinks and acts. He revealed what it looks like to live secure in a new *position* and revealed our new *potential* by powerfully pulling heaven to earth. Jesus was the perfect example of what it looks like to live *super* in the natural.

He had access to heaven's perspective. He walked in an intimate relationship with His Father and carried the power of Holy Spirit. And He purchased for us our *new position* and our *new potential* so, just like Him, we may have authority to access our *new power*. As children of God and as leaders, we have been invited to live with wisdom and revelation. We have been given authority to steward the power of God that we might use impossibilities as opportunities for the miraculous.

Jesus revealed the power of heaven when He healed, delivered, discipled and taught. The power of heaven destroyed the works of hell and the fruit was heaven established on earth. This life of power is the birthright of every son or daughter of heaven. We are designed to live secure as citizens of heaven that we might destroy the works of the enemy here on earth.

New power, like new position and new potential, has nothing to do with us and everything to do with God. He has done the qualifying by what He has done for and in us. Our access to our new power is always through surrender to Jesus. It is all part of the salvation package that begins and ends with His invitation to intimacy.

Jesus promised our new power just before ascending to heaven.

". . . you will receive power when the Holy Spirit comes upon you. And you will be my witnesses, telling people about me everywhere—in Jerusalem, throughout Judea, in Samaria, and to the ends of the earth." *(Acts 1:8).*

The word power comes from the Greek word *dynamis*. It means *strength, power* and *ability*.

Spiritual power is the release of the Holy Spirit through the use of spiritual gifts. These gifts of the Holy Spirit are described in Romans 8:4-8, 1 Corinthians 12:27-30 and Ephesians 4:11 as prophecy, faith, serving, teaching, encouragement, giving, leadership, kindness, miracles, healing, tongues, interpretation of tongues, evangelist and pastor. These gifts were revealed perfectly in the life of Jesus.

Through employing spiritual gifts, we access Holy Spirit power. Appropriate use of spiritual gifts links God's super to our natural—it's our new position partnered with our new potential, appropriating our new power on earth as it is in heaven. We have been invited to think, speak, and live from heaven's perspective. Holy Spirit power enables us to represent the works, the will, and the whereabouts of Jesus to the world.

Jesus told us that the Christian life was to be marked by power. But much like the training process of becoming an electrician who gains the authority to access power, there is a Kingdom process by which we access *authority* in order to steward our new power.

Authority

In the business world, where the bottom line is the objective, the words *authority* and *power* are often interchangeable. The more authority someone is given in the organizational structure, the more power he or she has to wield.

However, in the Kingdom of God, where *intimacy* is the objective, these two words represent a partnership between submission and revelation. When we submit to authority, we gain revelation and then we see how God sees. These actions empower us to pull heaven into every situation and, like Jesus, see the impossible bend its knee.

Authority, in a spiritual sense, is coming *under* something God wants us subordinate to so we can become qualified to steward power over something God wants redeemed. This principle is something that we see lived out every day in earthly governance.

As an Australian citizen living in North America, I am only qualified to have a position as a leader over an American church or business if I submit to, or come *under*, the authority of the requirements issued by the American Department of Immigration. If I do not submit to its authority, I am denied access to the opportunity to steward the authority it can give me.

We never have authority in our own right; we simply access it by living under the authority of Christ. Matthew 28:18-20 makes this clear,

Jesus came and told His disciples, "I have been given all authority in heaven and on earth. Therefore, go and make disciples of all the nations, baptizing them in the name of the Father and the Son and the Holy Spirit. Teach these new disciples to obey all the commands I have given you. And be sure of this: I am with you always, even to the end of the age."

The Greek word for all is *pas*. It means, *each, every, any, all, the whole, everyone, all things, everything.* Basically, all means all, and that's all, all means.

Jesus establishes He has *all* authority and then empowers us to live in it. It works like this: when we submit to the *all* authority of Jesus, we gain revelation of the Father's heart for His image bearers. You see, Jesus' command to "Go into all the world" comes after the statement regarding His authority.

God wants His sons and daughters to steward the authority of His Kingdom come in business. But we will not be given opportunity to access that *all* authority, unless we submit fully to the *all* authority of Jesus in our lives. True access to power is equated to true submission—it's how heaven thinks on the matter.

The implications are profound and observable. As we submit to God's all authority we gain access to Kingdom perspective and can therefore appropriate Holy Spirit power. As we live under authority we step into the all authority given to Jesus, and are empowered to unleash heaven into our areas of influence. This release is our birthright!

New power leadership requires surrender.

We were born to walk in power, but it must be accessed through surrender. If we circumnavigate submission to God's all authority, we will become fearful and abusive in our leadership. The power we end up wielding will be counterfeit to the Kingdom. Instead of our leadership encouraging and empowering those we lead, it will become caustic and harmful.

The Three Types of Leader—The DPR Paradigm

In my many years of pastoral ministry and coaching within the business community, I have witnessed many leadership styles and cultures. When it comes to the relationship between spiritual authority and spiritual power, I have witnessed three types of leader and the corresponding cultures each develops.

Decreasers

I have labeled the first type of leader as the *Decreaser*.

Decreasers are leaders who don't access their spiritual authority through submission to the all authority of Jesus. Therefore, they are not qualified to appropriate the spiritual power of the Holy Spirit. In other words, they are functioning completely in their own authority and strength.

Decreasers lead from *decreased* submission to the authority of God. This rejection of authority *decreases* God's supernatural power working through their lives, not unlike the experience of the Israelite leader Aaron, who, pressured by the people, sculptured a god out of gold. Aaron tried to meet a perceived need in his own authority and strength. It was a counterfeit to what God was doing through Moses.

Impatient for powerful results, the Decreaser will move in his or her own authority instead of submitting to God's. This individual will "take matters into his or her own hands." Decreasers are impatient. The immediacy of their needs causes them to operate outside of trusting in the goodness of God. While they believe that God can fix their problem, help them feel different, or make their dream happen, God doesn't move fast enough for their agendas or work how they think He should.

Decreasers rarely emerge overnight. They usually begin with a healthy understanding of God's nature and character. They love God, but, in the midst of the very real pressure to lead, they serve convenience, they choose the way of least resistance. They operate from "what seems right to a man." Because of this practice, their values and vision are subject to shift away from the values and vision of God until eventually their God is forged in the Decreaser's image.

This principle played out for me one day while working with a Christian business leader in North Queensland. In random conversation, he mentioned how he was having issues with his neighbor's kids. At first I sympathized with him. I too had some issues with a neighbor's kids taking things out of the back of my truck.

However, my sympathetic connection ended abruptly when I realized his issue and mine weren't even in the same universe; my problem was stealing, his problem was skin color! His Indigenous Australian neighbor's kids were playing "too close" to his property line; he needed to do something to keep them away from his family.

This Christian Decreaser had made God in his image and therefore he didn't view, nor did he want to view, that all people are made in the image of God. He actually felt justified in releasing his dogs on these children in order to keep them away from his property. In his words, "God wouldn't want his family anywhere near them!"

People are never in a place of stasis. They are either actively transforming into the fullness of the image of God, or actively deforming by recreating a god in their own image. My friend, Pastor Rob Buckingham of Bayside Church in Melbourne, Australia, puts it this way, "You can tell when people have successfully made God in their own image when their God starts hating the same people they hate!"

A Decreaser uses the idea of God to leverage the people under his or her leadership to gain advantage. Decreasers tend to consume the people they lead, as they would any other commodity. They believe those around them are there primarily to meet their needs. When those needs aren't being met any longer, the Decreaser will move on to the next victim.

The business life of a Decreaser is oftentimes marked by decision making without a compass. Moreover, leadership and way of life become governed either by a Decreaser's own arrogant belligerence, the loudest opinion in the Decreaser's ears, or the next fad or theory that permeates the cultural milieu of the day.

In this type of leadership culture, staff become frustrated with the direction in which things go. For the Decreaser, staff are there for one purpose only, to be tools in the Decreaser's hand to build the Decreaser's dream. People are simply commodities to be justifiably consumed by the Decreaser. Unsurprisingly, the compass of the Decreaser's heart is not aligned to the heart of the Father, meaning that vision, vehicles, and values shift with the changing whims of the Decreaser's perceived needs.

Decreasers never empower those they lead, instead they create cultures of fear and distrust and scheming.

I wonder if Paul had Decreasers in mind when he penned Colossians 2:8,

"Don't let anyone capture you with empty philosophies and high-sounding nonsense that come from human thinking and from the spiritual powers of this world, rather than from Christ."

If you find that your spiritual growth has been going backwards to the point where you no longer access your spiritual authority through submission to the all authority of Jesus, or appropriate the spiritual power of the Holy Spirit that you have been qualified for, you may be on the edge of Decreaser territory.

Policers

What about when a person accesses spiritual authority through submission to the all authority of Jesus but views God as controlling and authoritarian? A person in this position cannot appropriate the spiritual power of the Holy Spirit for which they have legal access to because they aren't operating in freedom. These leaders are called *Policers*.

Policers have gone after the authoritative command of the Great Commission without first following Jesus' instruction to wait in Jerusalem where "you will receive power when the Holy Spirit comes upon you . . . "

Policers tend to oscillate between need and fear—becoming spiritually bi-polar. They are in submission to God's all authority. As a result of their submission to our heavenly Father, He trusts them enough to reveal His heart to them. With the revelation of our Fathers' heart comes the revelation of the needs of humanity and a revelation of the mandate of a nations inheritance for King Jesus. The weight of this cosmic scale revelation to a Policer produces fear because the scope of the need and the mandate is greater than their natural abilities to meet it. Fear produces the need for self-protection. Therefore, for a Policer to feel secure, he or she needs rules, lots of rules to control natural ability outcomes.

Adherence to rules, to a Policer, demonstrates submission to the all authority of God because Policers don't have the evidence of the power of God at work to make such a demonstration. A Policer often says, "God is in control." What a Policer's actions say is, "God is controlling." And because adherence to rules equates to security for the Policer, the more intense the emotion of fear becomes, the tighter the control of adherence to the rules needs to be. For this leadership paradigm to function efficiently, it requires a controlling Policer to ensure the authority of his or her controlling God is adhered to, in order to demonstrate submission to God's all authority.

I have experienced many different leadership environments, both in business and the church. A Policer environment easily reveals itself to me without my talking to anyone. First it can be seen simply by the tone of the different types of signage. Start in the parking lot and you will see rules on display: "No Parking," "Stay Off the Grass," "Staff Only," and various others that point to people's organizational positions. In the lunchroom you can find signs that read, "Clean the Refrigerator," "Make Sure You Wipe the Counter," "Boss's Coffee Mug," etc. Signage in a Policer environment is negative and establishes a culture of adherence to the rules and reinforces positional control and authority.

It can also be seen in office layout. Control environments need hub-and-spoke relationships. Hub-and-spoke relationships will have the base level staff reporting as an individual spoke to a hub manager with little or no connection among each other. Cubicles for office staff that disallow eye contact are perfect designs for hub-and-spoke relationships to flourish. Where staff are mobile, then direct line reporting online is equally effective for maintaining an environment of control through hub and spoke.

Policers have no problem submitting to spiritual authority. The issue for Policers is the absence of spiritual power. There is no transformation without spiritual power. And Policers are terrified by true spiritual power because it has nothing to do with control and everything to do with freedom. Control is what makes a Policer feel safe.

Policers are prone to spiritual burnout and are driven by performance. They want to keep the approval of God, but they cannot meet the highlighted need of humanity revealed by God in their own natural ability alone. For a Policer, relationship with God becomes distant and performance based, driven by need, yet disconnected by fear. Policers don't have access to intimacy with God because they are afraid of Him.

I became good friends with one such individual. Warren and I initially met after I had preached on living in intimacy with a loving God. After the service, Warren made it very clear that He didn't believe in that kind of relationship with that kind of God. We set up a lunch so he could explain why I was wrong. I truly enjoy lunches of this nature.

Warren was a successful businessman. He had one of the most highly tuned business acumens I have ever seen. Talking to Warren, however, was like talking to a judge reading a verdict. I came to learn that while he was extremely fair in his dealings with all the people in his life, including his large staff, he was also unsurprisingly very controlling of every outcome in life and in business.

Warren's health was deteriorating, not aided by the fact he was carrying at least 50% more weight than would be considered healthy. At his own admission he had no relationships in his life that bought fulfillment and meaning, even though he was married with children.

Warren was drawn to me because, while I lived in the tensions of the corporate world, I wasn't striving and fearful. On the contrary, I walked with joy and peace. The Kingdom is righteousness, peace and joy in the Holy Spirit, and I had access to all three.

Over the coming months we connected regularly. One day Warren told me that he felt God was cracking the whip on him to produce more so that through his giving there would be more people in heaven. I had yet to convince Warren of God's loving nature, and so, Warren continued to live as the classic Christian Policer.

And I know so many, like Warren, who don't believe that God's power, through the work of Holy Spirit, is available to us today. I know so many who love God, but keep God and everyone else at arm's length, all because of the need to ease fear through control. I know so many who chose rules over intimacy and freedom.

Because Policer's are so controlling, they force the people around them, including family, into a relationship with rules rather than a relationship of intimacy and freedom with the Redeemer. Policers create a culture in their homes and businesses that puts God at arm's length, with lots of religious performance activity. In these environments, religious activity is an end in itself. Family and staff members of Policers oftentimes perform religious activity, such as prayer, bible study, attending service, to gain both God's and the Policer's approval.

A culture of performance in the workplace is produced by Policers, for the same reasons as stated above. Within the business environment however, physical resources can alleviate the tension for Policers between need and fear. Policers can mask fear, which is produced by an awareness of the scope of a *spiritual* need, by the satisfaction that comes as a result of their resource allocation to the exposed *physical* need.

In the Policer's business world, spiritual authority without drawing on spiritual power can lead toward philanthropy that is interventional and even preventative in nature, but stops short of spiritual restoration. The need is seen, acted upon, but the spiritual power necessary to bring spiritual transformation in the heart is not accessed, falling short of the fullness of the mandate of God to draw people into an intimate love relationship with Himself.

There are some incredible Policers in this world, doing amazing, never seen before acts of intervention and prevention, that heaven applauds. But they are only part way toward fulfilling the mandate of heaven as previously seen in Matthew 28:18-20.

You may be walking on the edge of Policer territory if you find yourself needing to control every outcome in your life in order to feel spiritually secure. And if you feel like God is distant, even though deep down you love Him with all of your heart, it may also be a sign of the same problem.

Releasers

Releasers are people who operate with both spiritual authority and spiritual power. Releasers are neither seeking to justify their actions like Decreasers, nor seeking to control outcomes like Policers. The Releaser is passionate about releasing the Kingdom of God in people and releasing people into the Kingdom of God.

The Releaser sees the need or crisis from heaven's perspective. They hear and know the voice of their heavenly Father and identify need, secure in their identity as a son or daughter. Need therefore takes the Releaser to a place of greater intimacy with God. Seeking out what His purpose is, in regards to revealing this particular need to them, opens up deeper levels of revelation concerning the Father's heart. Typically, Releaser's don't initially respond by trying to figure out what needs to be done about the need.

Craig Luper, Founder of Nehemiah International Ministries, sat me down in his office one day and we had what many call a "come to Jesus" conversation. I love those kinds of conversations!

He prefaced the conversation with, "Mark, you know I love you and have your best interests at heart, don't you?" I always shuffle in my seat when a conversation that is directed at me begins that way. "Yes mate,

I do." I replied.

"Well, I have observed your leadership up close and from a distance for some time now and I have seen some consistency in how you
approach new revelation from the Lord. I think you are seeking to operate in a new reality with an old paradigm."

"Okay, so you have my attention." I said. "What have you seen me
do?"

He continued, "Imagine being confronted with revelation from
God regarding a need in your environment. Revelation that creates an
awareness of need will provide you with an opportunity. Imagine you
stand in the entryway of a building that has two doors. You have the
power to choose which one of the two doors you can walk through."

"What are the doors called?" I questioned.

"The doors are labeled, *Figure It Out Room*, and *Council Chamber
of the Lord*. The observation I have made is that you consistently walk
through the *Figure It Out Room* door when revelation comes. You go
in there for lengths of time that range from a few days to a week. You
come out bloodied and bruised from slamming your head against the
brick walls in there, rarely, with any greater understanding than that
which you had before you went in."

The imagery was strangely akin to what I had been currently feeling. As a church planting pastor, I have had many opportunities to hit
my head against *Figure It Out Room* walls!

"He is right," I thought. "It is the first place I go. But why shouldn't
I? After all, I have been given a brain, and wasn't I responsible for my
part in being a good steward of *figuring out* how to apply God's revelation?" I relayed my thoughts to Craig.

He laughed and then said, "Yes, Mark. You are responsible, but
what if you only have part of the information before you start the
thinking process?"

"Go on," I said.

"In the *Council Chamber of the Lord*, you press in harder, sit longer,
and react with greater precision and with the full power of the Holy

Spirit working through you."

Craig was helping me in that moment to move from part Policer and part Releaser to become a fully operational Releaser. He knew I had a Releaser's heart. My heart was to release people into the fullness of all God had for them, but I was still using a Policer's pattern of behavior on myself and those around me in an attempt to control outcomes.

I became aware that, although I had a Releaser's heart, I was using people to build the dream, instead of using the dream to build people. When need would arise, I would use the ninety-nine to go after the one, instead of using the opportunity to go after the one to build up and release the ninety-nine.

Seasoned Releasers have discovered there is greater freedom to, and efficiency in, fulfilling the mandate of heaven to earth through empowering rather than controlling. It is the perspective of heaven regarding the children of God. Releasers discover a wonderful depth of intimacy with the Father because our Father is also a Releaser. Releasers live in a rhythmic love relationship with His heart.

Through Any Storm

My first job out of school was to join the Royal Australian Navy. As a sixteen-year-old, this was the adventure of a lifetime. I recall the first time I went to sea. We travelled from Melbourne to Sydney on H.M.A.S Tobruk. Tobruk was a flat-bottomed heavy landing ship. With a length of 417 feet and fully loaded weight of nearly 5,800 tons, she was no bathtub!

While traveling on my maiden voyage, we hit some pretty rough seas. For the seasoned sailors aboard, it was business as usual, but for me, the experience was terrifying. I had never encountered such tumultuous waters. One minute we appeared to be deep down in a watery valley with mountainous seas all around, the next moment we were soaring what felt like miles above the trouble. At times the waves appeared to be almost blocking out the sky. Then inside my belly I could feel a shift. I could feel this giant piece of floating steel begin to lift. And within moments we were once again atop one of those watery mountains and could see for miles.

I soon came to realize that the ship never did anything that the influence of the waves didn't permit. Tobruk never rose up when the waves were creating an environment for her to go down. And the reverse was also true. She was in perfect rhythm with the dynamic of the water surrounding her. The seasoned sailors understood this rhythm and experienced peace. If she were ever to get out of rhythm, it would signify disaster!

There are too many times I can point to in life where my heart was out of rhythm with my heavenly Father. I would be in the *Figure It Out Room*, trying to fit my rules of control around people and problems, while in the *Council Chamber of the Lord*, His heart was calling to mine, inviting me into deeper intimacy and connection, trying to show me a different way—release not control.

I would find myself going one way, while He was directing me another. All too often, I have found myself managing a pending disaster, when all along, I could have saved us all from stupid pain and increased my intimacy with Father God at the same time. My heart was right, but my paradigm was not.

But as I have leaned into becoming a Releaser, as I have committed to live in the *Council Chamber of the Lord*, I have found that my heart is at a place of the seasoned sailor. When issues come and storms rage, I am experiencing a peace I have not known before. I am better equipped to sense the *shifts* in our growth and development. I want to experience *rhythm* with my heavenly Father's heart on a daily basis such as that possessed by the likes of Charles Finney:

"The Holy Spirit . . . seemed to go through me, body and soul. I could feel the impression, a wave of electricity, going through and through me.

It seemed to come in waves of liquid love."

One of my deepest desires is to have my heart be in such rhythm with His heart that I can hear the subtle whispers of His voice in every situation, and then respond with the exact word, or touch, or prayer that is required at any given moment. And I want to lead from this place of security. Regardless of where we are in the waves, I want to empower and release those around me to live from heaven to earth.

Revelation

Operating from the *Council Chamber of the Lord* has influenced how I shepherd myself, as well as how I shepherd others.

When revelation comes, through either vision or problem, I can now hear the Lord say, "Let it breathe, and come closer." I don't have to control; I can trust, empower, and release.

As a young spiritual leader, the waves of revelation or circumstance seemed to overwhelm me. My submission to His authority was my primary focus. As a result, my attention was drawn away from stewarding His authority and power. For years I spent many hours oscillating between need and fear. This wavering kept me from leading with the confident faith needed to actually take hold of the authority and power of Holy Spirit. But the time spent in the *Council Chamber of the Lord* allowed me to enter into deeper intimacy with my heavenly Father and revealed greater clarity regarding the inflections and tones of His voice.

Because I have learned to wait patiently in the *Council Chamber of the Lord*, I have received the specific spiritual gift to deal with the specific issue at the specific time. Other times, I have been able to recognize the right word to speak, or identified the right help required, to meet the need in front of me.

Times in the *Council Chamber* have changed the practical steps I take in leading myself, my family and my team. Intimacy has provided the necessary *next step* to living in the fullness of my identity. My wife, Julie, recently completed a book on this subject entitled, "Boardroom of the Inner Man". I highly recommend this to you. It will help you maximize the time you spend with Father God in His *Council Chamber*. It will help you choose to step through the *Council Chamber* door instead of the *Figure It Out Room* door and provide you with a pathway to deeper intimacy with Him.

Conclusion

You are a precious member of God's royal family. He has no interest in keeping you at arm's length or placing you on a performance treadmill. When you accepted His invitation to join His family, He made some changes to your identity. You have a new position. You have new potential. And you have new power. It is what the perspective of heaven is concerning you.

Now it is time to be *released* to live in the fullness of all He has given you access to and to release others to do the same. He is calling you into His *Council Chamber* to breathe life into you, to prepare you to live in the reality of His Kingdom. The implications of walking in intimacy with God will affect you, your family and your business in very deep and profound ways. Are you ready to press on the correct door?

Your heavenly Father is in the Council Chamber and He invites you to enter in and sit a while. To "let it breathe." Your heavenly Father's desire is for you to walk in the fullness that is yours to access as a Releaser, a royal priest, a child of the living God. Give up your old way of thinking and begin to think how heaven thinks about you.

Press on the door and enter in. He wants to release you so you might become a Releaser.

4

What is Your What?

"When Christians say, "the Christ-life is in them", they do not mean simply something mental or moral. When they speak of being "in Christ" or of Christ being "in them," this is not simply a way of saying that they are thinking about Christ or copying Him. They mean that Christ is actually operating through them..."

—*C.S Lewis*

She Was Right

"I want to lock ourselves in our room for two days and fight like we have never fought before!" I blurted out. My wife Julie looked at me like I'd gone mad.

We had been making plans. Big plans. Attractions, beach time, reading time, pool time, shopping, and restaurants. We were headed on our tenth year wedding anniversary vacation, and it was going to be the stuff of legends. We were going to make sure our week away had a little bit of everything. This opportunity would become a high-quality mile marker for the narrative of our life together.

It was March of 2003 when my wife Julie and I had the opportunity to go to Alexandra Headland on Queensland's beautiful Sunshine Coast. Julie's parents had blessed us with a whole week in paradise and volunteered to mind our three kids. We couldn't wait to get started.

But I was feeling the need to get after something and I am not one for subtlety. I like cutting to the quick. I often make the bold statement so we can get to the heart of a matter. It's a part of how I'm wired. Julie fell in love with that man, and, she still loves that about me, most days…

"What?" She asked. Her expression not just suggesting I might have gone mad but also promising that if I hadn't she would.

I restated again, "I want us to lock ourselves away for two of our days and fight like we have never fought before."

"Ok. What are you on?" She exclaimed.

"I'm not *on* anything. I do, however, want to sit with you and spend two days writing down what it is we are trying to build together. I think there are things that you are building within our relationship that I am not, and things that I am building within our relationship that you are not. I want us to unpack what those things are and determine *what* it is we are building, and then determine *how* to build it together."

Looking back, it might have been better to lead with this.

You see, just a couple of weeks prior to what turned out to be a rather spectacular exchange, Julie had challenged me to think about writing a mission statement for our family. We had been in the process of writing one for the church and she pointed out how our family was of primary importance, and how we needed to be on the same page relationally at every level in order to know how to experience the quality of life we were capable of having—the life God has promised us.

She was right.

And that's all I was trying to say when I made my bold suggestion…

The fact is, I wasn't truly interested in fighting with my wife; I was truly interested in Julie and I better defining our *what*. The desire to lock myself away with her for two days, it wasn't about commitment, it was about unity.

There is nothing more frustrating than two people absolutely committed to each other moving out of unison. We had hit too many brick walls in the first ten years of marriage. There had been way too many unnecessary and painful misunderstandings in our lives simply for lack of a clearly agreed upon *what*.

It's very simple, you have to agree on *what* it is you are building if you want to build it together. While it is true that we needed to know *how* to move forward; *how* to experience full life together, we first needed our *what*, a mission statement, a set of plans...

Set of Plans

In the early 1990s, I worked as a leading electrician on building sites. One job I remember well was the construction of a large supermarket. We were given the customary drawings and schematics. Then the usual meetings ensued with project managers, engineers, and supply companies who were building some of the equipment for us to install.

The job was several months along the path to completion. Everything was going very well until one morning, I came in early to continue wiring an electrical sub-switchboard I had begun the day before. To my utter surprise, the door to the switchboard wouldn't open. To be more precise, it *couldn't* open. The ceiling contractors had been in during the night and installed thousands of square feet of ceiling. The problem was not that they installed the ceiling. That was expected and completed on schedule. The problem was the ceiling height. It was lower than the top of my sub-switchboard. Rather than stop and call somebody to clarify what was going on, they had just continued on their merry way, building my sub-switchboard *into* their ceiling!

I met with all the powers that be later that day. During the course of our meeting, we discovered there were two different sets of plans. The project manager had neglected to provide the ceiling crew with updated plans, and they had installed the ceiling based on the measurements of the incorrect plans. While the ceiling crew could have been a little more proactive, ultimately it wasn't their fault. They simply followed their "mission statement", without the overall picture of *what* we were all trying to build *together* in mind.

When I look over the landscape of Christian leadership, both in the church and in the business world, there appears to be several different sets of plans going around; plans on *how* to establish the Kingdom of God upon the earth. The problem is, there is little agreement on *what* that Kingdom looks like. And when the *what* is not clearly defined, the *how* often looks like ceilings installed too low.

Before Jesus ascended to heaven, He had one prayer in His heart, one passion, one instruction.

"I pray that they will all be one, just as you and I are one—as you are in me, Father, and I am in you. And may they be in us so that the world will believe you sent me." (John 17:21).

This was certainly a clear description of *how*. Unity is a high ceiling that will always get things done… But what things?

Jesus also gave us our *what* when He taught us to pray His Kingdom *"come on earth as it is in heaven."* And He showed us the *what* by the way He lived.

I would like to propose that the goal of a leader is to both clearly define the *what* and empower the *how* so we can all *get there together*. From my experience, the fullness of Kingdom living is not often realized in either the church or the business community because people aren't on the same page. This disunity leads to pain. But not the good kind, the other kind, it's called…

Stupid Pain

A *how* without a clearly defined *what* is a disaster waiting to happen. Just ask my biceps and quads every time I attempt to exercise.

In my youth, due to my own impatience, I operated in ignorance. I had seen other people get in shape, and it involved dumbbells and puffing. So, my faulty rationale was, if I picked up dumbbells and completed exercises that involved puffing, I too would be in shape. The idea being that activity equates to being in shape.

But of course, that's not fully how it works. And my biceps and quads let me know it. It's called stupid pain. And it's called that for a reason. Because it's pain that doesn't lead to gain. You see, I never really saw great results through my random acts of exercise and puffing.

The fact is, had I, in my youth, understood *what* I was attempting to do more clearly, then my *how* would have looked very different. I now understand that each muscle grouping requires particular attention in a particular order. Done right, you can lessen the risk of injury and stupid pain and experience the goal, gain.

Stupid pain gets you nowhere. It's the kind of pain that makes it impossible to climb stairs, get off the couch or even bend down to tie shoe laces! It is the kind of pain that causes people to slow down, become frustrated, or worse give up.

That said, there is such a thing as good pain. It looks like a couple, deeply in love, locking themselves away so they can determine their *what* together.

Good pain is the necessary pain that propels a person, couple, or organization closer to their goal. The more a person, couple, or organization experiences good pain, the closer the goal and the greater the motivation to press on. Good pain is what is experienced in a committed relationship with a clearly defined *what*.

There are many who have pursued Kingdom growth and hit avoidable walls. Many who have been spiritually injured and become disillusioned because of a lifetime of stupid pain; pain based on the puffing *how* activity that is experienced when we have a poorly defined *what*.

What does the Kingdom of God on earth look like?

The presence of Jesus…

The Divinity of God

The early church was Christocentric. Everything they thought and did was interpreted through the lens of the birth, death, and resurrection of Jesus Christ.

I believe we can best discover *what* the Kingdom looks like by reading what those who spent three years living with Jesus wrote. They saw Him at work, heard His incidental remarks, were witnesses to His interactions with people of all social classes, and they experienced the implications of His transforming teaching. They knew His presence.

The leaders of the early church were men and women with experiential understanding of the Kingdom. They walked with Jesus and saw the demonstration of heaven on earth. They witnessed His divinity; Christ as both fully God and fully man.

The Gospels are full of stories that reveal the divinity of Jesus. Maybe the best example is found in Luke chapter 5 where Jesus forgives a paralytic man of his sins before healing him.

The religious teachers of the law asserted, *"Only God can forgive sins"*.

To which Jesus responded, *"So I will prove to you that the Son of Man has the authority on earth to forgive sins."*

Then Jesus turned to the paralyzed man and said,

"Stand up, pick up your mat, and go home!" (Luke 5:24).

The early church leaders understood that any claim to divinity carried with it a claim to *all* authority. The definition of "all" is not complex. All means all and that's all, all means!

To the early church leaders and New Testament writers, Jesus as the second member of the triune, authoritative God, sits at the center of *what* the Kingdom of God looks like on the earth.

Jesus, as fully God and fully man, must be our starting place. *He* must be our *what* if we are to understand our *how*. Jesus *is* the set of plans. He revealed our *how* and it was very different to the ideas many of the religious leaders of the day thought. You see, Jesus revealed that the Kingdom was discovered in His presence not in a set of principles.

What Jesus demonstrated on the earth was a revelation of intimacy. He walked in unity with His Father and the Holy Spirit. He lived in a relationship with God and man and revealed that the Kingdom would operate the same way. His Kingdom come would be discovered in intimate relationship with God and then with each other.

Presence and Principles

"One day the Pharisees asked Jesus, "When will the Kingdom of God come?" Jesus replied, "The Kingdom of God can't be detected by visible signs. You won't be able to say, 'Here it is!' or 'It's over there!' For the Kingdom of God is already among you." (Luke 17:20-21).

Among you comes from the Greek word *entos*. It describes the nature of our relationship to the Kingdom of God on the earth.

The Pharisees were looking for a physical Kingdom. They sought a manifestation and establishment of political structures, principles, and rules that would set them free from Roman control and give them control over their way of life. Jesus gave them relationship and intimacy.

The word *entos* also explains both the geography and nature of the Kingdom of God on the earth. It is a relational term that illustrates proximity. It carries the meaning *in, inside,* or *within*.

In using this word, Luke purposefully ensured that the generations who follow would fully understand that the Kingdom of God on earth is a *person*, not a place. It is about encountering and knowing His *presence*; it can't be established simply through a set of principles.

Paul goes to great lengths in Colossians 1:13 to make this clear.

After he states that Christ *is* the centerpiece of the Kingdom of God on the earth, he describes our relationship to that Kingdom, *"For he has rescued us from the Kingdom of darkness and transferred us into the Kingdom of his dear Son."*

He uses the word *autos*, meaning *himself* making the conclusion that the Kingdom of God on the earth is not something possessed *by* God. Rather, the Kingdom of God on the earth is the presence *of* God in us.

Then, in verse 27, Paul lifts the veil of the mystery of Christ in us. *"And this is the secret: Christ lives in you. This gives you assurance of sharing his glory."*

Is it any wonder then that Paul, while explaining the rationale behind why he has given himself to the ministry of Christ, makes the well-known statement concerning our true identity?

"So, we have stopped evaluating others from a human point of view. At one time, we thought of Christ merely from a human point of view. How differently we know him now! This means that anyone who belongs to Christ has become a new person. The old life is gone; a new life has begun!" (2 Corinthians 5:16-17.)

The what of the Kingdom of God on the earth, therefore, is perhaps best stated as this: *people restored to God's original design and inhabited with His presence.*

The *principles* that Jesus taught are not the cornerstone of what we are building, rather it is the *presence* of Jesus Himself. Building relationship between people and God is the entire goal. Paul describes the nature of the construction of what we are called to build in Ephesians 2:20-21,

"Together, we are his house, built on the foundation of the apostles and the prophets. And the cornerstone is Christ Jesus himself. We are carefully joined together in him, becoming a holy temple for the Lord."

The building Paul describes is an eternal relationship that joins people to God across the span of the entire human narrative. And it does so through the eternal Christ as a reference point for the relationships to be built. The reference point is the purpose of the cornerstone. Once the cornerstone has been set in place, then all other stones laid are done so with relationship to the positioning of that initial stone. The moment we make principles the *what* and not presence, we move away from "on earth as it is in heaven" to "in heaven as it is on earth" because the reference point will have shifted away from Christ to our own selfish ambition.

I posit that by knowing the *what*, Christ in us establishing His Kingdom on earth by building people, drastically affects the *how*.

So, what are we building? We are building *people*.

Building People

The fact is, if our *what* is not about God's presence it will always default to being about principles. Leading from His presence is about relationship, it establishes His Kingdom, it empowers us into all authority. Leading from principles is about rules. It establishes law and dissension and creates a control-based culture.

If principles are always meant to come from relationship, from time in His presence, then principles to build people must be referenced in relationship to His presence. When they are, they will empower relationship and unity. When they aren't, they disempower and create discord and separation through a culture of control.

A leader has the power to make choices that will affect the lives of others. If you are a leader, then the lives you will affect as a leader will be both inside and outside of whatever system, structure, or business you lead. As a powerful person, you establish the *what* of your organization. You determine the vision. This will all be determined by how you view the people you are entrusted with to work toward the vision. The powerful choice you get to make is simply this: *Are you going to choose to use people to build the dream or the dream to build people? Principles or presence?*

If the Kingdom of God on the earth is about the presence of Christ in restored people, then building the Kingdom of God upon the earth and building people are one and the same thing and building a business or realizing a dream, is merely a means to an end, a vehicle to accomplish that *what*.

Leading your managers and staff from the *what* of the Kingdom of God changes the way you view those who are running with you in business. Applying this *what* will change how you view your time. It will change your decision-making at every level. Building a company or a business from this perspective will have ripple effects throughout your entire organization and will impact those you seek to trade or do business with because a Kingdom *what* will cause your business to become a genuine expression of the Kingdom of God upon the earth through you.

There is only one set of plans, one mission statement, under which all other *what's* must submit. As put before us by the early church, Jesus Christ is the centerpiece of the Kingdom of God. And He revealed that the Kingdom of God on the earth is the presence of Christ in restored people. Whether in church or business, our *what* is the same—build the Kingdom of God on the earth by building people.

Understanding that the Kingdom of God on the earth is the presence of Christ in restored people changes the way we view people. People *are* the building. People are the ones to be built.

This is the business of Kingdom business—building a big Kingdom by building big people with big hearts.

It took Julie and I until the ten-year mark of our marriage to figure this out. As you look at the plans of Kingdom-building, I hope our time locked away in a room in paradise fighting together clears up your *what* and provides you with a new metric to direct your *how*.

5

Building Powerful People

"Never look down on anybody unless you're helping them up."

—Jesse Jackson

It Takes One To Build One

While his name may never be spoken of in the great boardrooms of the major corporations of the world, nor his exploits be recalled among the political elite of society, my wife's grandfather personally impacted more people in positive ways than most.

A quiet man, Pastor Laurie, as he was affectionately known, was somewhat socially awkward in the presence of adults. However, his quiet authority commanded the attention of pupils in the rowdiest classroom environments. By the time he died in his early nineties, Pastor Laurie had travelled thousands of miles on his bicycle throughout the rugged terrain of southern Australia teaching religious education and Sunday School to thousands of children in the most remote areas of the state. He also individually impacted thousands of children throughout Africa using the "Mail Box Club" curriculum.

While living in Australia, random strangers, upon realizing my wife Julie was a grand-daughter of Pastor Laurie, would come up to her. They would tell stories of how they remembered him cycling into town with his home-made peddle organ, electric train sets, and flannel graph strapped to his bicycle. Some would recall how his presentations of the gospel, through the use of his many and varied creative devices, was the first time they had ever heard the message of a God who loved them and gave His life for theirs—changing their lives forever.

It takes someone powerful to build someone powerful. Powerful people build powerful people, and they use powerful tools to do that. Pastor Laurie was a powerful person in the eyes of heaven, one who understood the powerful tools of the Kingdom of God.

Those powerful tools are love, truth, and trust.

Love

Love is the appropriate response of a powerful person, made in the image of God, operating in the fullness of that image. In practical terms, this love looks like *respect* and *honor* toward God released through respect and honor for other image bearers. This looks like doing everything a restored, inhabited image bearer can do to help other image bearers of God live in the fullness of their image also. It looks like a quiet man revealing a magnificent God to a group of disruptive children in a remote classroom.

Paul the Apostle, in 1 Corinthians 13, gave us the great chapter that every couple I have performed a marriage ceremony for over the years, Christian or not, insists be included in their proceedings. Paul's dedicated chapter to the description of love lived out highlights love as the nucleus of a Kingdom relationship between God and people. Paul also opens his next chapter with the words,

"Let love be your highest goal!"

Just like Pastor Laurie, Christian business leaders have a powerful alternate metric at their disposal to measure success. We will look closer at this a little later, but for now it suffices to say that for a Christian business, the ultimate metric of success is not P&L statements, large salaries, or happy shareholders. These are all worthy pursuits and essential elements to staying in business. However, the perspective of heaven has determined that the ultimate metric of Kingdom success in any sphere of life, is love.

Love is not an option. There is no "opt out clause" to love. Love has to affect everything because it is the reality of the *presence* of the Kingdom of God on the earth.

Love is not a random or baseless emotion. Love is founded upon the essence of God's nature and character. John stated this notion in a beautifully and in a profound way in his first letter,

"Dear friends, let us continue to love one another, for love comes from God. Anyone who loves is a child of God and knows God. But anyone who does not love does not know God, for God is love." (1 John 4:7-8).

Nothing in all the world above or earth below affirms the image of God in another human being more than love. Nothing. Love is the most powerful tool issued by the Kingdom of God. With little more than a well-oiled bicycle and a heart filled with the love of our Father, Pastor Laurie respected and honored the children he was entrusted to speak to, and in so doing called out the true identity of a generation.

Love released through honor and respect, does not exist in isolation. Love is in direct relationship with truth and trust.

Truth and Trust

Jason Clark is a good friend of mine. We served together with several others on the senior executive team of a large church in Concord, North Carolina for several years. With around 40 staff and a volunteer base in excess of 200 people, I quickly came to learn that a large church is rarely problem free. There is always a relationship breakdown to resolve, a key crisis to respond to, a controversy that needs an answer, or a person who is just going squirrelly!

Each Tuesday morning, we would meet as a Team to discuss the week that had been and the week ahead. Yes, there were always wonderful things to celebrate and we did. But these weekly meetings were also the place where new problems would be presented and old problems would be discussed and monitored with regard to the progress toward resolution.

I began to observe Jason early on in our working relationship together. Each time a new problem would present itself, while the rest of us were either rolling our eyes, shuffling in our seats or holding back the urge to cuss, Jason, without angst, would sit back and smile. Sometimes he might even quietly laugh. Of all the emotional responses that might seem congruous with what we would be dealing with, smiling and laughing rarely seemed appropriate. It didn't exactly bother me, but I was curious.

I decided to take Jason to lunch one day to get to know him better. After our food order had been placed, football and weather discussed, I asked the question that I had been burning to ask. "Why do you laugh when we get a new problem?"

His answer sat me back in my seat and left me recognizing there was a significant void between my knowledge *of* God and my experience *with* God. He replied, "When we are confronted with a new problem, I see it as an opportunity to trust God in new ways. I simply cannot wait to see what my good Father is going to do in this new situation!"

Jason had successfully joined the dots between knowledge *of* God's love and experience *with* God's love, and the line that connected the dots is *truth* and *trust*. Pastor Laurie, like Jason, also lived with the dots of knowledge and experience joined by truth and trust. Stories are told of times he went, motivated by love for the children God had entrusted to him, to pay for the postage of his *Mail Box* lessons with no money in his hand. Each time he would be met by people, or find envelopes with the exact amount of money under the wiper-blades of his van to pay the required postage amount. For Pastor Laurie, his simple understanding and encounter with God's always perfect love produced an unshakeable trust based on God's truth.

To both these men, truth and trust weren't observations about God. Truth and trust were part of their encounter *with* God. They were both powerful people who created a culture around them that fostered the growth of other powerful people who came in contact with them. From the day I had lunch with Jason to this, I have made it my life's mission to think how heaven thinks by fostering the growth of powerful people through practicing what Pastor Laurie and Jason had learned concerning the relationship between love, truth, trust and the Trinity.

Here is how it works. . . .

Truth Trust and the Trinity

In John's Gospel, chapter 14, we find the essence of what Jason was talking about. Truth and trust from the perspective of heaven are revealed as the essence of the Trinitarian relationship between Father, Son and Holy Spirit. In verse 1, Jesus invites people in to an intimate trust relationship with the Father and then to Himself,

"Don't let your hearts be troubled. Trust in God, and trust also in me."

Trust is baseless unless there is a foundation of objective truth found. I discovered this reality the first time I put my full weight on a piece of sheetrock while working in a ceiling. I mistakenly thought it could hold my weight, but when my leg punched through to the room below I realized my trust was baseless!

Chapter 14:6-11 Jesus points to the objective reality that in the Trinitarian relationship trust is based on truth. Jesus not only reveals that it is the Father, motivated by love, who has directed the very actions they have seen, He declares that He, Jesus Himself, is the *personification* of truth,

> *"Jesus told him, 'I am the way, the truth, and the life. No one can come to the Father except through me.'"*

Jesus' invitation to trust is not baseless. As the personification of truth, Jesus *is* the basis of trust.

Jason not only understood the relationship between divine truth and trust as a theological construct; he understood it from a position of a love encounter. He accepted the invitation to participate in the divine relationship between truth, trust, and the Trinity. It's an invitation to encounter what we each have been offered, thanks to the role of the third member of the Trinity, the Holy Spirit,

> *"And I will ask the Father, and he will give you another Advocate, who will never leave you. He is the Holy Spirit, who leads into all truth. The world cannot receive him, because it isn't looking for him and doesn't recognize him. But you know him, because he lives with you now and later will be in you." (John 14:16-17).*

Perfect completion of the human experience can only be found in the encounter the Holy Spirit is seeking to lead us toward—a love encounter with the Triune God who is always perfectly truthful and trustworthy. The Triune God is in relationship with Himself and, as the only part of His creation made in His image, we too are designed on purpose for nothing less than full participation in this same relationship. The

Father sent the Son to look for a Bride who is wooed by the Holy Spirit. As a participant in the Triune God family relationship, trust becomes an encounter and not merely an expectation, because truth is a person, not a principle. That is why problems can be seen as an opportunity to trust God in new ways, and why Jason simply cannot wait to see what his good Father is going to do in new situations.

Divine love, truth, and trust in action is known as Kingdom authority. Kingdom authority produces a culture of freedom. However, authority mishandled is expressed as control and produces a culture of fear.

Here's why. . . .

Authority Verses Control

Divine love, truth, and trust are influences expressed as Kingdom authority. Manipulation is influence expressed as control by performance. Performance metrics manipulate an environment to produce a semi-predictable controlled outcome. Control is predicated on pride, as it assumes the environment or people are better off if they did things *my way.* For the son or daughter of God, pride is expressed as an attempt to take God off His throne, and replace Him with self. Pride says, "God doesn't know what He is doing and I do!"

My wife Julie has taught me that pride is a card-carrying member of the "Three Amigo's club." *The Three Amigo's* was a 1986 comedy that stared Steve Martin, Chevy Chase and Martin Short. It portrayed the story of three silent movie actors who were mistakenly identified as heroes in an impoverished Mexican Village, and together they had to prove their reputation.

Where pride exists, so does the other two amigos—judgement and unforgiveness. These three together masquerade, like the Three Amigo's in the movie, as guardians of our entitlements. Judgement decides for myself and those around me that, "I am right and you are wrong." And unforgiveness says, "because I am my own authority, and because I have the right to judge, I will not forgive you. I will not let you off the hook for what you did, because my judgement demands a punishment."

Control environments use people to build the dream instead of using the dream to build people.

Kingdom authority, unlike control, is predicated on humility. We see this seeming juxtaposition beautifully described in what has been considered a hymn of the early church in Philippians 2:1-11,

> *"When he appeared in human form,*
> *he humbled himself in obedience to God*
> *and died a criminal's death on a cross.*
>
> *Therefore, God elevated him to the place of highest honor*
> *and gave him the name above all other names,*
>
> *that at the name of Jesus every knee should bow,*
> *in heaven and on earth and under the earth,*
>
> *and every tongue declare that Jesus Christ is Lord,*
> *to the glory of God the Father."*

John Rowley was a leader who understood how to build powerful people via the relationship between authority and humility without the need for control. In the extreme tropical environment of North Queensland, Rowley could get men working at an amazing level of efficiency and speed. While it was typical in that environment for construction foremen to lord it over the workers, John's approach was very different. John would rather be in the trenches, quite literally, than stay in his air-conditioned work hut and drink coffee. He would even bring the site plans out into the field at times, set up a makeshift table out of an upturned cable reel and a piece of plywood, just to be with his men. On the times when there was a "big push" to get a job over the line, it was John who was the sweatiest, dirtiest and most worn-out of all who worked. First to arrive and always the last to leave, John would always slap the last guy on the back and say thanks as he left the site at the close of that day's work.

If anyone had a point of view pertaining to the job that was different from John's perspective, he would take the time to listen and consider, and, if it benefitted the safety of the men or improved the overall value and quality of the work, then he would implement the suggestion.

The result? No matter what John wanted, his workforce would bend over backwards to accommodate. If he needed anyone to go the extra mile, that person would in a heartbeat. There was never any dissension in the ranks. If there was anyone who spoke ill of John, the men themselves would bring correction to the disgruntled employee. Not even the Unions on site could do anything to put John's men off side with him.

John carried an undisputed authority every time he spoke, because of the relentless demonstration of humility he displayed every day. While John never mouthed the word "love," his actions revealed his true heart condition toward us. He genuinely loved his men. It was clear that John was under orders to get the job done; however, for John it was also equally clear to us that the job was a means to an end. The end for John was relationship with his men to help them be the very best they could be, and the job was just the vehicle to getting him there.

Love, truth, and trust are influences expressed through authority. Pastor Laurie, Jason and John Rowley lived this idea out intuitively. Real authority expressed in humility—not control.

Throughout history the people of God have had seasons of exceptional success exercising Kingdom authority through humility. Equally they have had embarrassing seasons of attempting to control everyone.

The Good and the Bad

A simple comparison between the early church of 165 AD to 266 AD to the church of the 15th and 16th centuries is a good example of the outcomes of these contradictory approaches.

Various communicable diseases ravished the empire of Rome during 165 AD and 266 AD, including the bubonic plague. The leaders of Rome were totally under prepared for how to deal with such mass death. It is estimated that somewhere between 25-to-30 percent of the population of Rome died during this time. Of note was the response of the Christian church. Rather than seek escape by fleeing the affected cities, Christians went *into* these cities to tend to the sick and dying at risk of their own lives. Charles Moore, in his article, "Pandemic Love," captured the essence of this part of early church history, when he wrote,

> *"In the midst of intermittent persecution and colossal misunderstanding, and in an era when serving others was thought to be demeaning, the 'followers of the way,' instead of fleeing disease and death, went about ministering to the sick and helping the poor, the widowed, the crippled, the blind, the orphaned and the aged. The people of the Roman Empire were forced to admire their works and dedication. 'Look how they love one another,' was heard on the streets."[1]*

While it is true to say that without doubt there were good men and women of God during the period of the 15th and 16th Centuries, sadly history has recorded that they were in relative short supply in the higher levels of the ecclesiastical structures. The excesses of the church are well documented during this time with the high level leaders functioning with political power, control and wealth, while the priests at village level were relatively uneducated and poor. The power abuses of the elite clergy during this era, would become one of the primary triggers for

---

1   http://www.plough.com/en/topics/faith/discipleship/pandemic-love

the Protestant Reformation that began with Marin Luther nailing his 95 thesis on the door of the Wittenberg Chapel.

If there is one thing the comparisons between these two distinctly different periods of church history has taught us, it is that Kingdom authority expressed through humility and fueled by divine love, truth and trust does not control, but rather creates a culture of freedom. A culture of freedom empowers a person to encounter the authoritative Christ, who lives in us, and this creates a culture that is ripe for revival. Control, on the other hand, seeks to strip an image bearer of God of his or her freedom to choose, and in so doing reduces a person to something less than what he or she was created to be. Control is the antithesis of Kingdom authority.

Fear or Freedom

Michael was a successful business leader at the top of his game. He loved God and even believed in a God who healed and blessed him. Michael was a difficult person to be in community with, however, because he always sought to control people and outcomes. His desire to control people and outcomes led him to become disrespectful to people and to those whom God had called into leadership.

One day, while sharing about his highly successful business, Michael revealed to me that he believed God was squeezing every little bit of life out of him, and was *"whipping"* him to produce more and more money for His Kingdom. He actually believed his personal health was connected to his performance!

It was little wonder that Michael had a hard time loving people unconditionally, and little wonder that his circle of friends was very small, and marked by people who either had the same view, or were easily manipulated to yield to his controlling ways. Just like any leader, Michael created culture around him. For Michael, the culture he produced was control, not freedom.

The Apostle John described Michael's culture in 1 John 4:18,

"If we are afraid, it is for fear of punishment, and this shows that we have not fully experienced his perfect love."

In all of the Bible, the only time a person is exhorted to control any person, is when control is directed toward self. Paul in Galatians, provides us with the well-known shopping list of Spirit fruit found in Galatians 5:22-23,

"But the fruit of the Spirit is love, joy, peace, patience, goodness, faithfulness, kindness, gentleness, self-control; against such things there is no law."

Lori and Scott Clifton, are the founding partners in a ministry based in Charlotte, North Carolina, called "The Inspire Network". I have heard Lori say on several occasions a truth surrounding these observations. She says, "Even on my very, very, very best day, the only person I can hope to control is myself!"

How Control Affects Us

The need to control arises from uncertainty about the truth of God's always loving character and nature. Doubt produces a lack of trust, insecurity and a false identity. It is the hallmark of a leader who operates out of principles instead of presence. If a person sees an authoritative God as a controlling God who controls people through fear of penalty and punishment, then insecurity rises up producing controlling behavior toward others. A culture of control by its very nature will always disempower people.

Seeking to control people is not only exhausting, it also creates a culture of fear. The belligerence required to manage a culture of fear produces anxiety and burnout in controlling leaders because most people simply don't like doing what they are told!

Understanding that our authoritative God *is* love, is perfectly truthful and trustworthy, produces a secure identity in the sons or daughters of God. If a person believes that the perfectly truthful and trustworthy God of love is in authority over them, then there is no need to seek control over any outcome or person, because nothing falls outside of God's loving authority. There is no need for fear or anxiety, because, as 1 John 4:18 puts it,

"Such love has no fear, because perfect love expels all fear."

Leading people through an encounter with Kingdom authority expressed through an encounter with His always perfect love, trust, and truth changes cultures from control to freedom. A Kingdom culture of freedom is the environment necessary for building powerful people. In a Kingdom culture of freedom people can explore, without fear, living out what it means to be a powerful person created as an image bearer of God. Freedom culture changes decision making at every level. Freedom culture changes the purpose behind conflict resolution. Freedom culture impacts those you seek to trade or do business with, because Kingdom authority will cause your business to become a genuine expression of the Kingdom of God upon the earth through you.

Perhaps your name may never be spoken of in the great boardrooms of the major corporations of the world, nor your exploits be recalled among the political elite of society. But there is one thing you do have the opportunity to be known for—that you took hold of the invitation to positively impact more people than most. Heaven thinks of you as a powerful person being called to build powerful people. You have been equipped with powerful tools to do that. Pastor Laurie, Jason and John understood it—love, truth, and trust. Humbly exercising

Kingdom authority to foster a culture of freedom.

part two

Speak Like Heaven

A person cannot accurately represent something until he or she firstly believes it exists and secondly, then seeks to understand it. That is why it is imperative to begin our journey together with thinking how heaven thinks.

Putting into practice the contents of the following pages will only have the impact on you for which you are designed if you are living from the perspective of heaven, made possible by time in His Word.

Learning a new language begins with a belief that the language exists and that it can be learned. It then takes intention and time. Learning to play the piano in front of large crowds required me to practice in a much smaller setting first and in the privacy of my own home before that.

Speaking the languages of heaven is much like that. Oh sure, there are the child prodigies who pick things up in an instant, but they are the exception, rather than the rule.

In the pages that follow, you are going to hear rationale and be exposed to, what for many, may be a brand-new paradigm. There will be subject matter that you may have previously distanced yourself from on purpose because you placed it in the *weird* basket.

I want to demystify the weirdness and place this conversation back on the pages of possibility. My prayer for you as you take a step on the journey to *speak like heaven speaks* is that you will come alive with the thrill that comes from gaining access to the spiritual tools that God, in His great love for you, has placed at your disposal.

Get ready to learn a new language, the language of heaven—a language of love.

6

God's Releasers

*"God is not silent It is in the nature of God to speak.
The second person of the Holy Trinity is called 'The Word'".*

—A.W. Tozer

Story telling has always run in our family, particularly on my Mum's side. I've been told my Grandmother would stand in the living room and regale family and guests alike with song, poetry, and story. Mum carried on the tradition.

From as early as I can remember she shared stories with us kids – stories of historic times gone by, of exciting childhood adventures, of funny experiences she'd had during the course of her day. She sang and wrote as well, poetry, and short stories. She authored several books capturing our local community and family history.

And like all storytellers, Mum was a wordsmith–she absolutely loved words. The origin and intent, inflection and presentation, words, they fascinated her.

She passed that on as well. I too, am fascinated by the origin, intent, inflection and particularly, the presentation of words. I've learned that the right word is better when delivered well. Tone and inflection can add depth of meaning to the simplest of words.

And then of course you have accents.

My accent is Australian, more precise, my accent is unapologetically rural Victorian Australian, or 'Straylyan'. My accent is very distinct.

Language and Articulation

One sunny May afternoon, I was about to participate in a breakout session at a conference in Redding California, when I heard someone call my name in a very distinct accent. I had just introduced myself to a small group in a hallway outside the conference room. A fella that happened to be walking by overheard me talking. He stopped and said, "Appleyard. You aren't 'one a th' Dumbalk Appleyards are ya? From South Gippy, Straylya?"

It had been years since I heard such a familiar and distinct accent. While the face was a little rounder, the crop of hair a little sparser, there was no mistaking, I knew the man.

"Steve Beaumont! Bowey! G'Day! Crikey mate... watta ya know?"

The fact is, I would have never recognized Steve but I could immediately tell where he came from by how he spoke. We were from the same rural Victorian community in Australia.

If you have ever travelled outside your region you have probably had this experience. You are in conversation with someone and then you stop suddenly because you overhear an accent similar to yours.

Language and articulation identifies, unites, and binds us. We all have a distinct accent, we all use words that uniquely express specifics of our emotions, will or desires. These words connect our past to our present and empower our future. Most importantly, these words help us define our story — our relationship with God and each other.

I believe that God speaks to us every day. He uses His written Word. But He also has distinct words unique to our relationship. We are in a relationship with Him and He loves us and lives inside us and I believe He uses fresh words to speak to us each day.

Like all healthy relationships, communication is of utmost importance in our relationship with God. Learning that God still speaks and learning how to recognize His voice affects every area of our faith.

The voice of God, what does that mean to you? What does His accent sound like, His articulation, His unique expression? How do you hear and understand Him?

I wish I could tell you my Christian journey into understanding the voice of God has been easy. I wish I could say I have always been confident that God spoke to me, that I consistently recognized and understood the voice of God. But it most certainly has not been the case.

My journey toward confidence in the voice of God has been more like running barefoot into a briar patch. I have spent years picking out thorns of criticism and poor theology from my feet so that I can be free to run again.

And So The Journey Began

I didn't accept Jesus' life, death, and resurrection as payment for the forgiveness of my sins until I was in my late teens. It was at a Christian youth camp. I am eternally thankful for the body of believers who unquestionably knew they were called to see people accept what Jesus had accomplished for humanity, and who explained it to me in a way that I could understand.

The newfound excitement I felt that day and the days that followed was overwhelming. I recall how immediately God appeared to me in visions and dreams, affirming my new identity. His voice in my heart was sudden, loud, and crystal clear. And I couldn't wait to share these fresh experiences with those who had taken the time to share the heart of my heavenly Father with me.

At one of our camp meal times, I managed to get a chance to share these things with the guest speaker of the camp. The expression on his face as I shared my new encounters with God told me that something was not right.

The more I shared about the things I saw and heard, the more furrowed his brow became, until he cut me short. With a sudden and rather abrupt tone, the type that school principals use when they have caught you doing something wrong, he said, "While I applaud your enthusiasm Mark, the enemy is trying to take you back!"

"What do you mean?" I asked somewhat defensively.

"Satan is trying to fill your mind with images and phrases and you are making idols out of them. You must not allow yourself to think or listen to these things anymore."

My excited heart sank in an instant and my joy and enthusiasm were replaced with fear and shame. Fear of an enemy who was *that* powerful, and shame that I would *allow myself* to do something that would undermine what the Lord had just done for me.

But there was also a puzzling question that began to form in the back of my mind. It found audience deep within my heart, "Why would God let His adversary speak directly to me. And why would God choose to only speak to me through His written Word. Why, after such an intimate first encounter, would He refrain from any other means of communication with me?"

And so my journey began.

Many years of listening, conversing, reading, observing, experiencing and doing have produced gloriously different conclusions regarding the way God speaks. I have come to know that the guest speaker, while sincere of heart, was devastatingly wrong regarding his conclusions about God's desire and ability to communicate. He held to a view of God that, while prevalent within the body of Christ still today, is in direct conflict with His character and nature. I have observed through God's workings in people and the world, and in my own life, that God is always speaking and we can know His voice, His inflection, His unique words.

The Silent Years

There is a period of time in the Old Testament known as the "Intertestamental Period," or "Silent Years." This is a period of approximately 400 years between the completion of the book of Malachi and the beginning of the ministry of John the Baptist. During this period of time there was not a single word from God. Not a peep. Nothing. Nada! All that the people of God had to go on was the Hebrew Bible, the Torah. The writings of the Torah spoke of the promise of a coming Messiah, which granted, instilled a measure of hope, but for 400 years the people of God were left guessing when He would come, as well as pondering whether He had forgotten them.

Generations never experienced God speaking directly into their situation. They longed for God to speak. Implicit with the promise of the coming Messiah was that God would speak again. This can be found in the book of Joel 2:28-29,

"Then, after doing all those things, I will pour out my Spirit upon all people. Your sons and daughters will prophesy. Your old men will dream dreams, and your young men will see visions. In those days I will pour out my Spirit, even on servants—men and women alike."

During the silent years the Pharisees and the Sadducees, two groups of religious leaders, grew in influence and power. In the absence of Gods voice, both groups sought control.

The Pharisees added to the Law of Moses through oral tradition, by creating 613 laws—365 negative ones and 248 positive ones. Adherence to these laws became more important to this group of religious leaders than the Mosaic law, and were designed to create a "hedge" around the Mosaic law to protect people from breaking it.

The Pharisees were classic "Policers." They created rules for everyone to follow, and they were experts at policing adherence to those rules. Pharisees understood the authority of God as presented through the Mosaic law, but they operated without the spirit of the law. Jesus pointed directly to this in Mark 3:3-4 before healing a man with a deformed hand on the Sabbath,

"Jesus said to the man with the deformed hand, "Come and stand in front of everyone." Then he turned to his critics and asked, "Does the law permit good deeds on the Sabbath, or is it a day for doing evil? Is this a day to save life or to destroy it?" But they wouldn't answer him."

The Sadducees were the powerful and wealthy elite. Their power was exercised through the Sanhedrin. They had reduced the Hebrew Bible to the five books of Moses, the Pentateuch. They rejected the other books of the Hebrew Bible.

They also denied the resurrection and were culturally aligned with the Greeks. Given their power base, they were a group of leaders who were very interested in keeping the status quo. This group of religious leaders would be closely aligned with today's "Decreasers." They placed earthy governmental authority above God's authority and operated without any recognition of the availability of spiritual power. They were spiritual skeptics. Paul, knowing the framework of their theology, threw a theological cat among the ecclesiastical pigeons in Acts 23:6-8,

"Paul realized that some members of the high council were Sadducees and some were Pharisees, so he shouted, "Brothers, I am a Pharisee, as were my ancestors! And I am on trial because my hope is in the resurrection of the dead!" This divided the council—the Pharisees against the Sadducees— for the Sadducees say there is no resurrection or angels or spirits, but the Pharisees believe in all of these."

So essentially the two groups of religious leaders that arose during a 400-year period of time when God did not speak were either hyper-conservative or hyper-liberal. Regardless, they had the same aim—control.

They did this by seeking to solidify their position between God and the people.

In church history, among those who believe God no longer speaks to us apart from His Word, I see a similar pattern. There are two groups of Christians—one hyper-conservative, the other hyper liberal. The conservatives build religious rules around the message of grace and freedom. The liberals seek to "reconstruct" the historical Jesus, leaving us with no relational Jesus at all.

Both the Pharisees and the Sadducees, in the latter part of the 400 silent years, controlled people to retain power and to ease the tension between a promise given and a promise not yet fulfilled. The need to control people and outcomes is largely based in insecurity, lack of awareness of true identity, and a lack of daily communion with God. The Pharisees controlled people through legalism. The Sadducees controlled people through politicking.

The Lie of Cessation

Controlling people are insecure people. They are greatly threatened by people who are free, people who live sure in their identity as sons and daughters of God. It then stands to reason that an insecure person's highest priority is to control those around them. If you wish to control an entire people group, you would start by suggesting that all of God is contained in the pages of a book.

Today there is a body of Christian leadership that no longer believes God speaks to the world apart from the written text of the closed cannon of Scripture. Known as Cessationists, this particular body of Christians also believes that the gifts of the Holy Spirit died out with the first century Apostles.

The gifts Cessationists particularly believe were shut down by God are the *sign gifts* of tongues, prophecy, healing miracles and faith. They believe these gifts were only given for the establishment of the early church. It is no accident that these are the only gifts Cessationist's believe have ceased because these are the gifts God gave that are the medium for His message apart from His Word. These are the gifts given so we can hear His voice, so we can know His accent, His articulation, so we can experience a relationship with Him.

At its base line, cessationism promotes an understanding that God has not spoken to His people apart from His Word for somewhere between 1500 - 2000 years. There are hyper-conservative and hyper-liberal Cessationists.

Cessationists argue that the ministry of the Holy Spirit, as described in the book of the Acts, is descriptive and not prescriptive; meaning that these writings were *describing* a series of historical events, not *prescribing* the activity of the Holy Spirit during these events as normative for every believer today.

When pitted against the nature and character of God, the Cessationist's view is in direct contrast to Scriptures that refer to how He interacts with His new covenant people. For example, God's sons and daughters are royal priests who have been restored. They host the presence of God in them. John 14:26 informs us even more about the nature of that relationship,

"But when the Father sends the Advocate as my representative—that is, the Holy Spirit—he will teach you everything and will remind you of everything I have told you."

I find the words *teach* and *remind* curious. They are the Greek words, *didasko* and *hypomimnesko* respectively, meaning, *hold discourse with* and *to suggest*. These words imply a personal interaction between one with information and another who needs that same information. It presumes dialogue, conversation, interaction. It assumes an exchange between two personalities.

Let's go deeper. In John 14:17, Jesus says this about the coming

Holy Spirit, who will live in us,

"He is the Holy Spirit, who leads into all truth"

Aletheia is the Greek word for *truth* meaning, *"truth in all its meaning and scope as embodied by Christ." (Vine's Expository Dictionary).* It is the same word used by Jesus in John 14:6 to describe Himself as "The Truth".

The Holy Spirit is not leading us to a set of moral or ethical principles, but rather to a *person* whose life embodies these moral and ethical principles, One who is the embodiment of divine relationship, who interacts, discusses, has opinions, emotions, shows love, and relates.

A Love Relationship

I have been a parent now for a little over 20 years. Before I became a parent I could have written love letters to my future kids. I could have created tomes of information; given them my thoughts regarding what is right and what is wrong. I could have helped to direct their decision making by giving them good principles by which they might navigate the waters of this world. And it would have been good, but to be honest, it would only have been necessary if I didn't plan on being around after they were born.

I didn't write those letters. Why? Because I stuck around after they were born. I am actively involved in every aspect of my kid's lives. We live in the same house; we talk, we eat together, pray together, laugh and cry together. I dream with them and lovingly discipline them. I'm there for them when they are in need and I always will be. It's called relationship and it's something I highly value with each of my children.

Honestly, Cessationist's paint God as an absent father; a distant, stoic, emotionally unavailable God. Psychologists would say this type of emotional distance between fathers and sons, or fathers and daughters, is detrimental to developing emotionally healthy and stable adults. No kidding!

But that is not the Father Jesus reveals. The relationship between Father, Son and Holy Spirit, is a highly relational one of love. And we are invited into that same relationship!

"This is real love—not that we loved God, but that he loved us and sent his Son as a sacrifice to take away our sins. Dear friends, since God loved us that much, we surely ought to love each other. No one has ever seen God. But if we love each other, God lives in us, and his love is brought to full expression in us. And God has given us his Spirit as proof that we live in him and he in us" (1 John 4:10-13).

Acceptance of the invitation into this divine relationship of love releases our true identity as sons and daughters. We are created to be loved by God and to love Him in return, and to love others also. It is a love relationship. And like all the best relationships, it involves a great depth of regular communication between both parties.

I wonder how long my relationship with my wife would have lasted if after our wedding night I declared, "Now that we have been legally married in the eyes of God and man, and now that we have truly become one flesh, I believe it would be detrimental to our relationship for me to talk to you. I have written some love letters to you, so that you will understand for all the ages to come just how I feel. I have listed them in chapter and verse to make it easier to memorize. Just read those for about thirty minutes each day and you will understand my heart and my plan for our lives together—I love you!"

Then silence.

Can you imagine the great insecurity that reality would release in our marriage?

My wife didn't marry me to just be one flesh with me and to have a secure future. She married me for a *love relationship*, a daily dialogue, the intimate sharing of hearts and dreams, the interaction of personalities and love.

Think for a moment of the Bride of Christ as a metaphor of the church's relationship with the Triune God. Would a relational God who is in perfect in relationship with Himself, design us in His image for a love relationship with Himself, and then be a silent partner in the lead up to a cosmic marriage between us, His Bride, and Himself?

Of course not!

To suggest God only interacted with His people just long enough to establish the necessary literature containing moral and ethical principles is to suggest His one ambition is to save our souls. Of course He wants to save our souls, but from the beginning He has wanted so much more, an intimate love relationship with us. We are His kids, His sons and daughters created in His image, to be in a love relationship with Him.

What we believe about how God communicates has a significant impact upon our identity. If our relationship has its beginning and end in a salvation experience, if He stops speaking after we give Him our hearts, then we will become greatly insecure. Insecurity will influence our theology, which in turn influences our actions and reactions toward God, our family and our work colleagues.

If we live insecure we will become threatened by people's freedom and we are then more likely to limit opportunities for freedom to be exercised. We will also become prone to be more intent on ensuring people are placed in relationship with the religious rules instead of a love relationship with a liberating Redeemer. We will likely become Decreasers or at best Policers.

Believing God doesn't speak today apart from His Word, that He no longer has gifted us to reveal His power, reduces our freedom to live as royal priests, sons and daughters of heaven. Not unlike the Pharisees and the Sadducees, it is a theology of control through reduction of spiritual freedom.

Salt Shakers, Pepper Shakers, and Coffee Cups

One morning I was sitting in my favorite coffee shop just outside of Charlotte, North Carolina. A Jewish friend of mine was with me seeking to know the difference between what he had observed in Julie's and my ministry over a couple of years, and what he had observed in so many other spiritual leaders' work. He was struggling to understand how we, as ministers of religion, functioned day to day with people, because he saw we had no interest in controlling people.

On our table was a saltshaker and a peppershaker. I bought them to the center of our table and placed them some distance apart. I said, "Imagine the peppershaker is God and the saltshaker is God's people."

He nodded. Taking my coffee cup, I placed it in between the saltshaker and the peppershaker.

"Now, let's assume this coffee cup is the minister, priest, rabbi, whoever you want to imagine as the religious leader. Typically, they place themselves in this position between God and people because they are the religious 'experts,' and because the people are dependent upon them to interpret what God is saying through His Word."

He quickly agreed. I continued, "This is the most dangerous of positions for a leader, it should never happen! From the coffee cup position, a leader can make God sound like anyone he or she wants Him to sound like. It is a position of extreme power, influence, and potential manipulation."

I then took the coffee cup and placed it *alongside* the saltshaker representing God's people.

"This is the position Julie and I do our best to place ourselves in. We choose to coach people, to run the race with them, to help them learn the art of listening to His voice for themselves. We coach them to read His written Word, so that when He speaks through the gifts, they know the kinds of things He says. When they ask me what I think about a situation I usually reply with, 'It's not about what I think! Let me help you learn to hear His voice for yourself so you can know how He thinks, then you will hear with great clarity and peace.'"

The alarming thing for Julie and I is God's people continually try to place us in the position between the shakers. It is easier for people to have us positioned there. People don't have to think for themselves when spiritual leaders are placed in between themselves and God. People feel less accountable with a *Coffee Cup* positioned between themselves and the *Peppershaker*. When spiritual leaders are placed in between God and people, it is easier to find someone else to blame when things go wrong. It feels safer to take frustrations out on Coffee Cups than Peppershakers.

Placing people between yourself and God creates a very unhealthy spiritual atmosphere on many levels. Not least of which is the unhealthy atmosphere of codependency. For the follower, they get their security not from God but from their leader – that's scary. And let's face it, for the leader it's just a whole lot easier to get the follower to do what needs to be done.

God Is Speaking Today

Another point of consideration pertinent to this discussion of cessationism: if indeed, God did cease to speak apart from His Word and remove His gifts from the body of Christ, when exactly did it take place?

Was it the exact moment the last period was placed at the end of the last canonical book? Was it the moment the Damasine Council of Rome in A.D 332 or the Council of Carthage in A.D. 397? Or was it after A.D. 500 when it is supposed that all of the Greek speaking church at last accepted the finalized list of the Old and New Testament books?

Certainly, if cessationism is to be consistent with its own arguments then the evidence the early church fathers use to support their case, such as the writings of Irenaeus (d. 202) and Origen (d. 254), cannot come into play. The two church fathers, Irenaeus and Origen, loosely claimed that God had already stopped speaking and they died many years before the other councils I just referenced convened.

And if God ceased speaking apart from His Word before the Greek church accepted the writings around A.D. 500 then the writings of Chrysostom (d. 407) or Augustine (d. 430) are equally invalid.

Are you confused yet? Exactly.

What about all the people in the New Testament who spoke in tongues, prophesied, performed miracles, and healings? What happened to them? One day, they were operating in the gifts and actively hearing God's voice, and the next morning they woke up and... nothing; the silent years all over again? Masses of God's people who just moments before had an intimate love relationship with Him, now no longer could hear His voice or see His power, and even worse, they had no access to His written Word, because Guttenberg wouldn't build his printing press for another thousand years!

If such a catastrophic event had happened in the Body of Christ, there would be ample literature available to note it. No such literature exists.

If God ceased to speak to His people outside of His written Word, then the only access to God's voice we as believers would have would be totally dependent upon Coffee Cup preachers; those leaders who position themselves between God and the people in order to interpret His Words.

They are called Decreaser's and Policers, or Cessationists.

Cessationists ultimately cannot be Releasers. They simply cannot partner with heaven to see God's Kingdom come.

Paul makes it clear when he writes about the reality of a believer's new position - there is to be no Coffee Cups between God and us,

"But whenever someone turns to the Lord, the veil is taken away. For the Lord is the Spirit, and wherever the Sprit of the Lord is, there is freedom. So all of us who have had that veil removed can see and reflect

the glory of the Lord. And the Lord who is the Spirit—makes us more and more like him as we are changed into his glorious image" (2 Corinthians 3:16-18).

There are significant implications pertaining to what we believe about God's character and nature and how it relates to our own identity as sons and daughters. I believe Paul summarized it best in his letter to the Galatian church chapter 3:3-5,

"How foolish can you be? After starting your new lives in the Spirit, why are you now trying to become perfect by your own human effort? Have you experienced so much for nothing? Surely it was not in vain, was it? I ask you again, does God give you the Holy Spirit and work miracles among you because you obey the law? Of course not! It is because you believe the message you heard about Christ."

It is my firm belief *and experience* from over twenty years of practical ministry in different nations and contexts that God does in fact speak fresh words today. He is the ultimate Releaser. He stands supreme in the area of sacrificial pursuit for the hearts of humanity. He lived, died and rose so we wouldn't need a Coffee Cup between Him and us. He purchased for us access to an intimate love relationship with Himself.

He has a timeless message that He wants to bring to the world, and He wants to use *you* to deliver it in a way that is congruent with your own unique personality, experiences, skills set, and networks. It will involve you pressing in deeper to His Word, and deeper into His heart than ever before, and allowing His love to speak directly into every area of your life and leadership.

One thing is for certain, what He says and reveals to you will always line up with His Word because He is,

"...the same yesterday, today and forever" (Hebrews 13:8).

And as Paul's second letter to Timothy informs us in chapter 3:16,

"All Scripture is inspired by God and is useful to teach us what is true and to make us realize what is wrong in our lives. It corrects us when we are wrong and teaches us to do what is right."

As already established, He doesn't lie.

God is speaking today—right now. In the following chapters I want to introduce you to the Kingdom tools of love, the gifts of the Holy Spirit, attributes God has given you access to so you might hear and know Him.

God has given these tools to the body of Christ… to you, to equip and activate you to speak and release the language of heaven. To *speak what heaven speaks* upon the earth. God has called you to be a "Releaser." He has something to say to the world today; a message; fresh words for this moment, to release to your world. He wants to say it and release it through you!

7

A Lesson in Love

*"If you know that God loves you, you should never question a
directive from Him. It will always be right and best. When He gives
you a directive, you are not just to observe it, discuss it, or debate it.
You are to obey it."*

—*Henry Blackaby*

A Red Bike And A Boy Named Jimmy

If you had asked my Mum whether she moved in the gifts of the Holy
Spirit, she wouldn't have known how to answer. We grew up Cessationist—believing that spiritual gifts such as speaking in tongues,
prophecy, and healing ceased with the original twelve apostles.

But, whether she acknowledged it or not, she was as natural in the
use of some of the gifts as any person I have seen. It was a rushed trip to
the old pizza shop where I first realized this fact; where my Mum taught
me a powerful lesson on love.

In 2011, Mum visited us in North Carolina from Australia. It was
a three-month visit and we did it right. Lots of touring, and food, so
much food! She tried everything from hot wings to candied yams, Cow
Tails (a brand of caramel candy that is wrapped around a cream center) and, of course, good old North Carolina barbecue. We were doing
our best to give her the full experience of life in the "South". But it was

while waiting in a pizza shop at approximately 6:30pm on a gray, rainy November evening that Mum gave me the most powerful of gifts—a revelation of love.

It's helpful to know a little of Mum's background before I dive further into this story.

Her trip to North Carolina was not just about seeing the world and eating southern staples; it was also an opportunity to find some healing of her own deep wounds. Dad had passed seventeen years earlier, and Mum had never fully recovered. Then, just before her visit, she had to confront the sudden passing of both an adult grandson and her own eldest son.

After raising seven children, Mum worked as an in-home caregiver to the elderly and children with special needs. Love was her life. And she gave it freely and it cost her something. When you love deeply, you feel loss deeply.

At 76 years of age, Mum was still pretty spritely. She wasn't about to be left in the car while I collected our pre-ordered pizza.

It was a small pick-up area—two seats squeezed up against the wall between the window and the front counter on the left, and standing room only between the door and the drinks fridge four feet away on the right. And that night there were at least 10 other hungry American pizza lovers waiting in front of us.

If you know me, you would know that in high demand seasons of life, patience is occasionally in short supply—this was one of those high demand times. It had been a full day, I was hungry, I wanted to be home and eating.

I *may have* succumbed to impatience. As I turned away from the counter to take a deep breath, so as not to give my frustration away, I realized I had *lost* Mum! How could I, a well-educated leader of a complex organization, possibly loose a septuagenarian in a room not much bigger than an oversized pizza box?

I looked right. I looked behind. I looked two deep in front of me, but no Mum. Then I saw her hidden. No wonder I had missed her. She was crouched down, wobbly knees on the floor, looking intently into the face of a special needs child aged around nine years. I immediately noticed the young boy's mother was wiping tears away from her eyes. I pushed my way through the fellow impatient pizza waiters and got to Mum just in time to hear her say to this grinning young man,

"Jimmy? Wow, what a strong name for such a strong young man."

Then Mum said something amazing. "You look like the kind of young man who loves the color red and who likes to ride his three-wheeled bike fast down mum and dad's driveway. Is that right, Jimmy?"

Jimmy's eyes were the size and brightness of two shiny silver dollars as he turned his head toward his teary mum, his head nodding furiously in confirmation to what this aged agent of love had just released. But it was Jimmy's mum that grabbed my attention. Teary eyed, she confirmed the red three-wheel bicycle.

Then Mum, with her gaze fixed on the young boy's face, simply said, "God loves you, Jimmy." Then, turning her face toward Jimmy's mother, she said, "God loves you too, mum."

Then, with no fuss or fanfare, she simply took my hand to steady herself as she got back to her feet, asked about how much longer the pizza was going to take and made her way back to a seat near the door.

And I realized in that moment, that while I was focused on pizza, my Mum was putting on a Kingdom clinic. She displayed to all of us, in a most excellent way, what love does. And, whether she knew it or not, she used a gift of the Holy Spirit to speak out on the earth a conversation that was taking place in heaven. With the very simple "red, three-wheeled bike" and "God loves you," she gave a word of knowledge. She was speaking what heaven was speaking. This word changed the atmosphere of earth by releasing the atmosphere of heaven.

My Mum had used a *Kingdom tool of love*, a *word of knowledge*, to do what every gift of the Spirit does, reveal God's always perfect love.

Even So, the Gifts Are for Today

I refer to the gifts of the Holy Spirit as *Kingdom tools of love,* because I want to be clear about how I define their purpose. It's about love, always.

I am aware that many have seen or experienced the gifts of the Holy Spirit mishandled by the body of Christ. These gifts have been misused at times to manipulate emotions or to promote personal agendas. They have not been about love. And I am aware that these practices have led to the gifts of the Spirit being associated with those "weird people" who swing off ceiling fans when the church music starts or connected to questionable methods that lack sound reason and rationale.

I am aware of these associations because I, too, have seen the gifts misused.

Like power tools in the hands of untrained people, the gifts of the Holy Spirit when misused cause damage. Just a cursory glance at church history over the past 150 years will reveal great abuses and damage. Damage to people's hearts and people's spirits, damage to relationships, churches, and wallets. As a Cessationist, in the first 10 years of my ministry, I was acutely aware of these misapplications. I went out of my way to look for them, and there were plenty to be found.

I have seen its ugly abuses in many forms. From pastors who manipulated financially vulnerable parishioners with promises of financial breakthrough if they would up their giving, to business leaders who use fear and shame as spiritual principles to motivate their team to perform better.

Yes, there have been obscene abuses by immature people *pretending* to have the gifts of the Holy Spirit. When spiritually immature people try and influence others his way it can come across as spiritual elitism.

The sad irony is, at times, Cessationists have used the mounting examples of church leaders masquerading as carriers of the gifts of the Holy Spirit as opportunities to warn would-be inquirers that Satan works through gifts, instead of people. I know, because I was one of them, and I had plenty of audience with other clergy who felt the same way.

My wife, Julie, is currently (as of December 2016), in the process of writing a book entitled, *Journey to Brave*, about the years of transition we embarked on as we evolved from Cessationists to a son and daughter operating in the fullness of the gifts of the Holy Spirit. Her book, when completed, will serve as a trail of breadcrumbs left purposefully along the path to encourage others to follow.

As a person who has experienced the power of our good God through the responsible use of His good gifts, I now see a different picture. I now know that we are called to use these gifts to speak how heaven speaks. I have observed, time and again, that responsible use of the gifts of the Holy Spirit will *always* draw people into deeper intimacy with Him. As I have trusted God more with His good gifts, I have seen what I helped for a long time to propagate—that keeping people away from the true gifts of the Holy Spirit leads to a decrease in intimacy with God in the Body of Christ. It leads to Policer and Decreaser dominated environments in church, family, and business.

1 Corinthians 12:4-6 is one place that shows the proper connection between the gifts of the Holy Spirit and intimacy with God,

> *"There are different kinds of spiritual gifts, but the same Spirit is the source of them all. There are different kinds of service, but we serve the same Lord. God works in different ways, but it is the same God who does the work in all of us."*

As we have seen previously, the word *in* is the Greek word *en*, meaning *in, by, with*. Paul establishes that through the use of gifts, the work of God will be functioning *in* us, *by* Him, and *with* us. To disallow the use of the gifts of the Holy Spirit in our lives is to refuse to permit a particular function of God to be released in us, by Him, and with us. It is to decrease the opportunity for intimate partnership with Him.

The fact is, the gifts of the Holy Spirit are for today!

The Sign Gifts

The gifts of the Holy Spirit are Kingdom-building tools that release the conversation of heaven upon the earth. Paul lists them in 1 Corinthians 12:8-10 and 14:1-11. While several of the gifts are more pragmatic in nature, such as teaching, pastoring, administration etcetera, some of the less practical gifts I particularly want to focus on are what I refer to as the "*sign gifts.*"

The sign gifts are words of knowledge, words of spiritual wisdom, tongues, prophecy, faith, healing and miracles.

In the coming chapters, I will focus on the sign gifts. My purpose is two-fold.

First, I believe re-establishing these gifts within the Body of Christ, in particular, through the Christian business community, will produce greater Kingdom results for the same effort already expended.

Second, I believe, for the most part, even the most ardent Cessationist would agree that gifts of teaching, administration, pastoring, and evangelism still exist today.

I believe the sign gifts demonstrate beyond a shadow of a doubt that the supernatural has invaded the natural—the conversation of heaven can be heard. There is rarely any natural explanation when a sign gift is released over a situation or circumstance. But when we walk in the sign gifts, we walk in supernatural authority and power to see His Kingdom established in the lives around us and the areas of our influence.

A great example of this is the story of Simon the Sorcerer, found in Acts 8:9-11,

"A man named Simon had been a sorcerer there for many years, amazing the people of Samaria and claiming to be someone great. Ev-

eryone, from the least to the greatest, often spoke of him as "the Great One—the Power of God." They listened closely to him because for a long time he had astounded them with his magic."

But now the people believed Philip's message of Good News concerning the Kingdom of God and the name of Jesus Christ. As a result, many men and women were baptized. Then Simon himself believed and was baptized. He began following Philip wherever he went, and he was amazed by the signs and great miracles Philip performed."

When the *true* power of God comes, this power highlights two things: there is a "super" to be experienced beyond our "natural", and the counterfeit of God's true power is exposed.

Words of Knowledge

For the remainder of this chapter, I want to explore the first two of these sign gifts, the Kingdom building tools of love. *Words of knowledge* and *words of spiritual wisdom* are two gifts that give a believer the ability to speak the language of heaven—to communicate how heaven speaks.

Words of knowledge are very specific. They are divine revelations given by Holy Spirit that speak the conversation of heaven directly into a moment of specific need.

Words of knowledge come to people who have no previous awareness of the specificity of what is required to meet a particular need. It is Jimmy and his mum knowing that God sees and truly loves them by hearing the words, "Who likes to ride his three-wheeled red bike fast down mum and dad's driveway." They are words that mean very little to nearly everybody else on planet earth in that moment, yet reveal to a specific person that right there, right then, that they are seen, known and loved by God.

It is important to recall what Paul said about the origin of the gifts of the Holy Spirit in the first part of 1 Corinthians 12:4,

"There are different kinds of gifts, but the same Spirit is the source of them all."

The gifts of the Holy Spirit are the Holy Spirit Himself, so what He says will be consistent with who He is.

A wireless microphone reproduces exactly what is spoken into it. It requires real power to operate, and it needs to be tuned in to the correct frequency and must be in close proximity to the voice it seeks to reproduce. Words of knowledge work exactly the same way. They require real Holy Spirit power, a heart that is tuned into the conversations of heaven through the Word of God, and a person who is intimately connected with God on a daily basis.

A wireless microphone doesn't paraphrase or interpret what is said by the voice speaking into it. It is an exact representation of the voice. A person who delivers a word of knowledge is simply to do just that. Deliver the exact word.

As with all of the gifts of the Holy Spirit, it cannot be overstated that the metric for accuracy of the word as being a word *from* God, is the Word *of* God. God will never contradict Himself. It is not in His character or nature. So, it is good practice to ask the question of a person you do not know, who has a "word," how often that individual is in "The Word." It is also good practice, if you are still becoming familiar with Father's voice, to take the "word" you have received and measure it against His Word for yourself.

Speaking in front of people multiple times every week for more years than I can remember has provided no shortage of unusual situations. One Sunday, during a message I was delivering, a crackle came over the PA system and a local cabbie began having a conversation with his boss. Thankfully there was no cussing! The words that came through our PA system in no way matched up with what I was saying.

There were two conflicting messages coming to the ears of the people. And most importantly, the people knew it, because they knew the sound of my voice and they knew my heart of love for them.

God uses words of knowledge to talk *through* you to reveal exactly what He wants to say *to* others. In doing so He reveals something very specific into a situation that says to the recipient, "God sees you right here, right now".

Gods deep desire is to involve His children in the process of bringing His will in heaven to the earth through His communication to the world. It is clear when it is not Him, because it doesn't sound like Him. It doesn't line up with what He typically says. It doesn't reflect His heart of love.

When we discover how much the Father loves us, our hearts are drawn to His. God loves and wants to reveal His heart *to* us and *through* us.

Words of Knowledge Always Sound like Our

Father's Love

I enjoyed some of my youth spending time with my dad fishing. The tangled lines, the old bait stuck to the bottom of the boat in the scorching Aussie summer heat, the smell of dead fish, they were all part of the fishing experience.

Fishing's central purpose is to draw fish near to your line and your boat so they can come into the proximity of the hook. In the Gospel of John chapter 6:44-45, Jesus, who we well know commissioned the disciples to become fishers of men, said,

"For no one can come to me unless the Father who sent me draws them to me, and at the last day I will raise them up. As it is written in the

*Scriptures, 'They will all be taught by God.' Everyone who listens to the
Father and learns from him comes to me."*

The Father draws us near to Jesus. He does so by revealing His
love for us. He wants to talk *to* us, He wants to talk *through* us! Words
of knowledge is one such way that He does just that. Using the gift of
words of knowledge tunes people's hearts to the voice of the Father. A
genuine word of knowledge moves our attention from the general to
the specific. It gets our attention in an otherwise distracting world. It
brings the atmosphere of heaven into overcrowded pizza joints.

And *you can* hear what heaven is saying! It is not possible in the
natural, only in the spiritual. In both Romans 8:16 and 1Corinthians
6:17, we are told that we now have a direct line connected with God,

"But the person who is joined to the Lord is one spirit with him."

Our spirit is joined as one with Him. Jesus told us Holy Spirit would
lead us into all truth. Words of knowledge is, therefore, a means for
God to make known a specific truth otherwise hidden. It is a powerful
Kingdom tool of love in the hands of the builders of the Kingdom of
God. It provides us with the supernatural means to bring the conversation pertaining to what heaven thinks in a specific moment, to specific
people, in specific circumstances.

Words of knowledge can help a person see what is blocking their
relationship with God, what things are holding them back from what
God wants for them. Words of knowledge reveal His truth in a very
specific way, bringing affirmation, support, comfort, and encouragement.

I was once watching a teacher in a classroom of a primary school in
Australia. The class was rowdy, and the rambunctious boys were doing
their usual stirring up the girls and hitting each other.

Rather than do what I would have done, screamed for everyone to
sit down and shut up, our teacher spoke quietly. She used tones that

drew the boys and girls towards her. She used words of affirmation and words that called out their true identity and drew them near. One by one the students quieted and gathered until they surrounded their teacher, and the room was still enough for all to hear every word she spoke.

One thing is certain, words of knowledge will always draw us to the Father because if they are from God, they will always come from a place of love and speak to our true identity as sons and daughters of heaven.

Words of Spiritual Wisdom

Words of spiritual wisdom is the next gift of the Holy Spirit for us to look at that is closely linked to words of knowledge. Both are found in 1 Corinthians 1:8,

"To one person the Spirit gives the ability to give wise advice; to another the same Spirit gives a message of special knowledge."

The only time I enjoy slapstick comedy is when it is not rehearsed but actually happening in real life. . . .

My future in-laws lived in Bowen North Queensland, a transient rural village of fishermen and fruit pickers. Bowen has a small hospital, a high school, a few stores, and, of course, the Bowen Fire Department. My father-in-law was one of the town medical doctors, and he and his family lived in an apartment on the main street of town above the medical clinic they ran.

One evening we were all sitting around talking when suddenly my future brother-in-law yelled for everyone to join him at the window.

"The Grand is on fire!"

The Grand View Hotel was situated on the corner of Herbert and Dalrymple streets right across from what was then the Herbert Street

Medical Clinic.

Flames were everywhere. People were running outside from the downstairs bar with beer glasses still in hand, helping those, who just moments before, were their drinking companions, as they climbed from the upstairs balcony, safely to the street below.

Then came the sirens. The old Bowen Fire Department fire engine screamed down Herbert Street, lights flashing and bells ringing. Men in older style fire suits hung off the side, the back, and the top of the Engine, as they pulled up alongside the Grand View.

And then the real show began!

Did I mention I love slapstick humor, but only when it's happening unrehearsed?

The fire truck was suddenly crawling with bar patrons holding beer glasses, the precious amber fluid spilling over. Trying to be helpful, one would-be firefighter took hold of the giant coil of hose, and with several of his Aussie mates, preceded to unravel it. Holding one end, they walked up and down the street looking for where the hydrant might be located. After a brief discussion and lots of finger-pointing, they decided to look back next to the fire truck. Sure enough, success. They all let out a cheer!

The truly exciting part was what came next. One man attached the hose to the truck at the same time as another man turned on the water. This pairing of activities came in perfect concert with a third man who turned on the diesel pump. No one let the fourth man know what was happening. Who was the fourth man? The one with a beer in one hand, the hose nozzle end in the other. He was in deep conversation about who knows what with several other "firefighters."

The water could be seen traveling at an alarming speed down the hose toward "Number Four." I almost wanted to cheer, it was such a good show.

The pressure hit 'Number Four' and firefighters one through three let out several creative expletives as the beer glass flew out of Four's hand and his feet left the ground. I think I did laugh then.

The other firefighting companions did their best to take hold of Four, trying to wrestle him, the hose, and their beer glasses all at the same time. Meanwhile, the water seemed to be hitting everything except its intended mark! After the fact, it was determined, with little surprise to anyone, that the water did just as much damage to the building as the fire....

Well-meaning Christian people share their "wisdom" with the world every day. Just look at social media. Everyone is suddenly a spiritual philosopher, theologian, business guru, all with wise thoughts to shower upon the world.

Out-of-control *spiritual* people throw what they believe to be God's Words on everyone. When we endeavor to speak to the world's problems with words of wisdom that aren't spiritual words of wisdom, we oftentimes cause more harm to people than the original problems—especially if we speak from wounds and disappointments.

A husband and wife came to me one day clearly upset. Their marriage was walking on the edge of self-destruction. They had decided they needed to get some good Christian counseling, so they went to a lady who advertised to provide such services. They sat down together on one side of the office desk, this Christian counselor sitting on the other. They told her the answers to her appropriately probing questions.

After acquiring the answers to her questions, she said, "Well this is a slam dunk." Pointing to the man she said, "You are just like my first husband. You two need to get divorced!"

Now this is not a book to talk about the rights and wrongs of marriage relationships and divorce, but suffice it to say this was an out of control fire hose—a person giving "spiritual wisdom" from a place of hurt.

So, what are words of spiritual wisdom?

Colossians 3:2-3 provides us with a good starting place,

"Think about the things of heaven, not the things of earth. For yo died to this life, and your real life is hidden with Christ in God."

Speaking what heaven speaks starts with thinking what heaven thinks. Pastor Wayne Cordeiro put this idea best when he said, "Wisdom beyond your years is gaining answers to questions you don't know how to ask yet."

True words of spiritual wisdom will always call out people's true identity as sons and daughters of heaven, and will always call people toward deeper intimacy with our heavenly Father.

Words of spiritual wisdom are dependent upon the transformed mind of Romans 12:1-2. In other words, words of spiritual wisdom will never contradict heaven's perspective. We are told we have the mind of Christ in 1 Corinthians 2:16,

"For, 'Who can know the Lord's thoughts? Who knows enough to teach him?' But we understand these things, for we have the mind of Christ."

The renewed mind, the mind of Christ that is ours, will be a mind that thinks thoughts and speaks words in line with the fruit of the Spirit. If you haven't learned them yet, now is a good time to memorize them. They are found in Galatians 5:22-23. I have also thrown in verses 24-25 for free!

"But the Holy Spirit produces this kind of fruit in our lives: love, joy, peace, patience, kindness, goodness, faithfulness, gentleness, and self-control. There is no law against these things! Those who belong to Christ Jesus have nailed the passions and desires of their sinful nature to his cross and crucified them there. Since we are living by the Spirit, let us follow the Spirit's leading in every part of our lives."

107

rected fire hose, words of spiritual wisdom can forgiveness with words of love, the flames of an- e, the flames of mistrust with words of kindness. dom target the lives of people with these spiritual fruits to call out their true identity by expanding their view of their current situation.

Roger

Roger is a successful businessman whose entrepreneurial skills and intuition have allowed him success in many arenas of business ranging from property to clothing to music. As I sat with him one day, he shared some of the issues he was having with his children. They were great kids, but just would not do what he told them to do!

"I just don't get it," he said, "I can run a businesses with employees, and work with bankers and developers. I have no problem getting any and all of these people to do what they are told, when they are told to do it. When there is any push back, we work through it and arrive at creative solutions. No problem! So why is it that I don't see the same results with my kids?"

"Great question, Roger. Right question, Roger," I said. "Tell me about how much time *you* spend with your kids."

"Well, we go on vacations. We go out each week as a family to eat, and I sit and have dinner with them most nights of the week. I work hard to provide for them and make sure they want for nothing. I tell them regularly that I love them. Surely they should respect and obey what I say, because surely they know I have their best interests at heart."

"I think you are making a false assumption, mate," I stated.

"What do you mean?" a puzzled Roger questioned as he sat himself forward in his chair.

"You are assuming your positional authority as your children's father gives you the right to speak into their lives."

"Well, of course it does! Doesn't it?" he asked.

I responded, "Roger, you need to earn the right to speak into their lives as much as you do with every other human being on this planet. So I ask you again, how much time do *you* spend with your kids? God is calling you to be the primary male figure in their lives who helps them to hear what heaven says. You are the one person on planet earth that can show them a healthy image of their heavenly Father. Heaven is calling you to a new set of priorities because heaven has a greater perspective of your identity for you to see."

Roger then invited me to help him with some of the specific changes he needed to make in order for him to embrace this transition in his life, so he could walk in the fullness of his identity.

This conversation released words of spiritual wisdom into Roger's life that were calling Roger toward his true identity as a son of heaven. These words of spiritual wisdom shone a light on the reality that he was the one who had been entrusted with the most amazing responsibility of being his children's father. He couldn't delegate out that responsibility and expect to build a culture of love in his home at the same time. Only he could do it. God designed it that way. And the gift of words of spiritual wisdom was given by God to help him to see the bigger picture and achieve the fullness of his calling.

Expand Your Horizon

Mount Stewart is a large rocky bluff on the outskirts of Townsville in North Queensland, Australia. It is a popular place for crazy people who like to hang like spiders off thin pieces of rope many feet off the ground. I'm not fully sure of how my friend Craig convinced me that it was a good idea to participate in this activity, but late one summer's afternoon, participate I did.

Craig and his brother, Dwayne, were seasoned rapellers. Craig pulled the straps tight around my nether regions as he harnessed me to the rope at the top of the mountain. Dwayne prepared to belay (secure) me from the ledge way below.

Tunnel vision set in the moment I stepped near the edge of the cliff face. My back turned, my shaky boots perched nervously on the edge, with pebbles and small rocks releasing from the edge of the cliff face. All I could see were my hands clutching the rope . . . with every fiber of my being. All else appeared dark.

Dwayne encouraged me from below to trust him and press off from the top. With my eyes closed tight and my cheeks puffed out, I took the leap. I felt the rope strain tight and sensed the pressure of the harness around my body as my weight began to be fully supported. I was encouraged to launch out again as my feet embedded themselves in a new resting place further down the cliff face. Two more times, and I was located about halfway down the bluff. With growing confidence, I prepared to push off again when Dwayne yelled out for me to stop, let go of everything, turn around, and take in the view.

With a newfound sense of trust in his expertise and the equipment that was well supporting me, I let go. Swinging my body weight around, I opened my eyes. Tunnel vision had passed, and suddenly I saw a vista that has etched itself into my memory forever. Magnetic Island, Palm Island, and a few smaller islands were so close I felt I could just reach out and touch them. Their shores were being caressed by azure waters that grew a deeper orange by the minute as the sun's fading rays reached out for one last kiss on the landscape. The warm tropical breeze brushed my face on its way along the mountainside, and the sounds of seabirds coming back to shore to nest for the night were crystal clear above the sound of the cityscape below.

My horizon was expanded that evening. I needed to trust my friend's wise word that he had me and that the equipment was strong enough to support me. I had to *presume* the wisdom of his experience. And it was only then that I was able to take my eyes off my circumstances and see the fullness of the view before me.

God has gifts for you to apply in your personal life, your business, and your church, so He can expand the horizon of your identity and empower you to walk in the fullness of His always perfect love. Words of knowledge and words of spiritual wisdom, when used as they are designed to be used, are powerful Kingdom tools of love that will grant you access to that new horizon.

Sometimes this access will be as simple as God's love being revealed by telling Jimmy and his Mum about the color red and riding bikes. Other times it will be a father such as Roger coming to the realizations that to operate in the fullness of his identity as a son of heaven, he needs to be a fully present father on the earth.

The gifts of words of knowledge and words of spiritual wisdom are there for you to take hold of today. Don't delay. Begin speaking how heaven speaks into your family, your staff, your board. God wants to speak about His love *to* you and *through* you, in order to draw you and others closer to Himself and see you affirmed and walking in the fullness of your identity. This is the beginning of *how* to build the *what* of the Kingdom of God. The goal in church and business is the same goal—the presence of Christ in restored people.

Trust God with His sign gifts and you will gain a whole new perspective. He will expand your horizon. It's the perspective of heaven and the view from there is breathtaking!

8

Totally New Kind of Normal

"In these last days when God is pouring out His Spirit in great cloudbursts and tidal waves from the floodgates of heaven and the great river of life is flooding our spirit and body and baptizing us with fire and resurrection life and divine energy, the Lord is doing his acts. His strange acts, which include dancing in the Spirit and speaking in other tongues and many other operations and gifts. The Holy Ghost is confirming the last message of the coming King, with great signs and wonders and miracles."

—Maria Woodworth Etter

Turning Your Natural Strength Super

In the long hot tropical Queensland summer of 1994, I was subcontracting my electrical services to an electrical installation company that specialized in mining equipment. Everything was big. The equipment we installed was big. The tools we used were big. The amount of food we ate to fuel our bodies—big. Even the bugs that bit us were big!

Late one afternoon we found ourselves on a big job installing a high voltage power cable to power a big 24 kilovolt electrical transformer. Things were going as planned until we encountered a *big* problem.

The air-winch we were using to pull the cable began to lose traction—the cable was too heavy. The air-winch was supposed to pull the cable but just the opposite was happening. The cable was pulling the air-winch. As a solution, we decided to attach the air-winch to a neighboring concrete wall. We pulled out the industrial sized rotary hammer drill and bolted the air-winch to the wall. We were excited and just a little bit proud of ourselves for coming up with such a creative solution to our *big* problem.

We fired up the air-winch again. Before long, the straining sound turned to popping sounds as the winch broke free of the big bolts we had used to secured it to the wall. Our problem moved from big to *very* big. Even with the proper tools, the sheer weight of the cable made it simply impossible to move. We needed a new strategy.

We each began to process ideas.

"I got it!" Gary, my creative workmate, said.

"Let's grab Johno's ute, tie the air-winch to it and drive it over the embankment."

Johno was our boss. A *ute* is the affectionate term Australians use for a pickup truck. We had "borrowed" our boss's brand new ute earlier in the day to haul equipment to our current location. We still had it.

Our job site was situated along a dirt driveway about fifty feet above the natural landscape. The drop-off from the road was not ninety degrees, but nearly. It was certainly too steep for a boss's brand new ute to be used like a pendulum.

"That's a great idea!" I said.

We secured the ute to the air-winch with heavy duty cable. Then we drove the ute over the embankment.

It worked brilliantly.

The ute provided the necessary counterweight to stabilize the air-winch. We moved the impossibly heavy cable to its desired final resting place smiling the whole time. We leveraged our resources and suddenly what was impossible with sheer strength was possible. With little effort, we moved thousands of pounds of cable. . . .

Jesus – Making the Natural Super for All of Us

There are gifts of the Holy Spirit that God has given to His children that are designed to take the natural, and make it *super*. In short, God's speaking to us strengthens us. These supernatural gifts provide so much spiritual strength that they are able to make impossibilities possible. These gifts shift atmospheres and circumstances against the spiritually resistive forces that oppose them.

And there is opposition. . . .

These gifts make it possible for us to live a totally new kind of normal.

Jesus famously said in John 14:12,

"I tell you the truth, anyone who believes in me will do the same works I have done, and even greater works, because I am going to be with the Father."

Greater works will be done. That's what Jesus said. And He wasn't suggesting; He was promising. It poses a great question. How can natural people do greater works than the supernatural Son of God?

One of the most amazing things about Jesus is that while He was *positionally* fully God, He set many of the *functional* elements of His divinity aside to become fully human. If Jesus had performed all His miracles as God, He couldn't expect us to *do greater works*. My point, Jesus performed miracles as fully man in God, as fully son in His Father.

I learned classical piano for most of my growing up years. I am reasonably accomplished and given a full-sized grand piano, I can make it produce beautiful music. If I am given a small toy keyboard with a dozen or so keys, I am incapable of producing the same music I can produce on a grand piano due to the limitations of the instrument placed in front of me. In this situation, my *position* as a musician hasn't changed, because my ability hasn't changed. My *functional* boundaries have.

Paul gives us a glimpse into how this example relates to Jesus in Philippians Chapter 2:6-7,

"Though he was God, he did not think of equality with God as something to cling to. Instead, he gave up his divine privileges; he took the humble position of a slave and was born as a human being."

Jesus placed the functional boundaries of humanity around His divinity. He became the perfect archetype of a human living in the power of the Holy Spirit totally dependent upon Father God. He demonstrated what it looked like to live naturally supernatural and He purchased for us access to that same life. In Christ, humans are designed to function supernaturally.

The gifts of the Holy Spirit are given to us to think, speak and live like Jesus. They take the natural and make it supernatural. The reason we can do *even greater things* is because our Father, in His goodness, gave the gifts of the Holy Spirit to His children.

The fact is, God commissioned us to the impossible task of establishing His Kingdom upon the earth. Then He provided His sons and daughters with the supernatural resources of heaven to match this responsibility.

In the natural, what we are called to do is impossible. There are resistive spiritual forces against us establishing the Kingdom of God upon the earth. We do not have the strength in and of ourselves to perform such impossible tasks. No amount of natural energy or effort will produce the required result. An attempt to live minus the supernatural gifts will ultimately lead us to live from either a Decreaser or Policer paradigm.

Unless the sons and daughters of heaven access the particular gifts of the Holy Spirit that provide the spiritual strength necessary to move situations, atmospheres, and circumstances against the spiritually resistive forces that oppose them, there can never be total mission accomplishment.

We Are in a Fight

There is a battle. We are in a fight. There is an enemy who seeks to keep us living always overwhelmed by the natural. We are contending for one of two cultures—hope or fear.

This is an inner battle with outer ramifications. As a leader, you know that your inner culture will become your outer. If you walk in peace, hope, and trust then it will be evidenced when the time comes where peace, hope, and trust are needed.

The gifts of the Spirit are given to empower your inner culture so your outer culture matches. The fact is, you give what you got. If your life isn't marked by the gifts of the Holy Spirit, your leadership will be marked by striving, control, and ultimately fear.

And while it is of utmost importance to say yes to all the gifts God has given, it's also good to understand how the enemy will seek to keep us focused on the natural.

Peter understood the strategies of our enemy and our need for strength. In 1 Peter 5:8-9, Peter says,

"Stay alert! Watch out for your great enemy, the devil. He prowls around like a roaring lion, looking for someone to devour. Stand firm against him, and be strong in your faith."

It is important to expose the tactics of our adversary, the schemes of the enemy, so we may access the good gifts God has given to His sons and daughters and be filled with the necessary spiritual strength to establish the Kingdom of God upon the earth.

Schemes of the Enemy – Attack the Supply Line

Napoleon Bonaparte was once recorded as saying, "An army marches on its stomach." He understood that steady supply lines carrying food and weaponry were imperative if his troops were going to succeed on the battlefield. In fact, he once offered a prize of 12,000 francs to anyone who could develop a way of preserving food for his troops. This challenge led to the modern methods of canning and preserving food that we use to this day. Logistics in warfare are often at the very core of whether victory or defeat is experienced.

In modern warfare, even with all of the advancements in technology and tactics, the basics remain. A good defensive strategy includes protecting and growing the strength of your own supply lines, while a good offensive strategy includes disrupting and weakening your enemy's supply lines. Why? Because when you disrupt your enemy's supply lines, you weaken your enemy's strength by weakening their capacity, capability, and resolve. In short, you tamper with their hope of victory.

If you were the spiritual enemy of God and you wanted to stop the advancement of His Kingdom upon the earth, and you knew what spiritual gifts His sons and daughters required access to in order to be strong enough to oppose you, what would you do?

You would do all that you could do to deny them access to those strengthening gifts!

Our spiritual enemy actively seeks to disrupt the supply lines that strengthen the sons and daughters of heaven. He accomplishes this feat by delegitimizing the gifts of the Holy Spirit that have been given by God to strengthen us—the gifts that release the conversations of heaven upon the earth. By removing our strength, he tinkers with our hope. When we are in a place of spiritual weakness, the promise of a greater works existence seem further away and our faith is undermined. Or maybe a better way of articulating it is, our faith is placed in the wrong thing.

We all have an inner faith life, an inner culture we are developing in everyday life. Hope and fear are two opposing cultures. Fear is faith in the wrong thing. Fear is faith employed in the belief that bad things will happen. Hope is faith in the right thing. Hope is faith employed in the belief that promises will be fulfilled, promises such as "greater works."

Schemes of the Enemy – Divide and Conquer

Another strategy used in warfare for hundreds of years is the "divide and conquer" strategy. *Wikipedia* explains the divide and conquer strategy well,

"Gaining and maintaining power by breaking up larger concentrations of power into pieces that individually have less power than the one implementing the strategy. The concept refers to a strategy that breaks up existing power structures and prevents smaller power groups from linking up."

Our enemy likewise employs the same strategy within the body of Christ. He has stirred up dissension; the gifts of the Holy Spirit have become a point of division, two camps within the church. Then, within each of the two camps, he has created finer points of disagreement to further divide each from the other, acts that ultimately result in a powerless church.

But we are not powerless.

Revival and the Business Community

The gifts of the Holy Spirit are given to develop a hope that ignites faith on a scale never experienced before in this generation. As our hope is realigned with heaven's agenda of establishing the Kingdom of God upon the earth, we will see people restored to relationship with Him. I believe this generation stands at the precipice of what will be the greatest revival the world has ever seen.

And I believe the business community is recognizing this quicker than the church community.

I believe the business community is recognizing the need for the super to partner with the natural, that releasing the conversations of heaven into day to day realities is an imperative to Kingdom advancement. They sit on the front lines of philanthropy and humanitarian crisis, and they see that the natural capacity to meet the supernatural need is insufficient. There must be an infusing of the super with the natural.

I am seeing the business community in this generation already taking the lead by taking hold of all God has for them. There is a rising tide of desire in the business community around the world to add God's super to their natural in order to overcome opposing forces that stand in the way of mission completion.

The Gift of Tongues

Ephesians 6, the most concise chapter about spiritual warfare, has been preached on and written about by many men and women with more degrees than a thermometer. And yet oddly, the key dot that joins the appropriation of the spiritual armor to the human experience is rarely joined. That dot is *"be strong."*

"Finally, be strong in the Lord and in his mighty power" (Ephesians

6:10).

If you think about it, to tell a natural person to "be strong" by themselves in a super way is as absurd as expecting a snail to "fly" because you told it to. There must be more to Paul's instruction; an invitation to discover *how* to access who we are in God.

The Greek word Paul uses for *strong* is *endynamoō* meaning *to receive strength.* And the word *kratos* is used for *mighty power,* meaning, *force strength.*

So, it reads something like this. *"Finally, receive strength in the Lord so you can force strength."*

Where do we, natural people, go to gain access to such super force strength?

Do we *receive strength* from going to church; from the worship songs or our pastor's words? Do we *receive strength* from performing yet another philanthropic or religious task? Is *that* the kind of strength Paul referenced?

I believe that we receive strength through the gifts of Holy Spirit. I believe the kind of strength Paul wrote about, strength that will enable sons and daughters to overcome opposing spiritual forces and live a totally new kind of normal here on earth, is found in the gifts.

The first gift I want to go after here is the gift of tongues. It will be the focus of this chapter. The gift of tongues is given to strengthen us on a personal level. It is Holy Spirit strengthening our spirit, by speaking to our spirit in a spiritual language.

"For if you have the ability to speak in tongues, you will be talking only to God, since people won't be able to understand you. You will be speaking by the power of the Spirit, but it will all be mysterious... A person who speaks in tongues is strengthened personally..." (1 Corinthians 14:2 & 4).

Paul reveals that the supernatural language of the Spirit is not something that can be manufactured by natural means. The very speaking of it is mysterious and can only happen when the super meets the natural, via the power of the Holy Spirit.

Paul describes a language with words mysterious to us. He uses the Greek word, *mystērion*, meaning *ordinary mortal men will not be able to understand.*

Luke wrote in Acts 2:1-4, that the gift of tongues pertains to the speaking of earthly languages as well.

"And everyone present was filled with the Holy Spirit and began speaking in other languages, as the Holy Spirit gave them this ability."

The one constant is that the gift of tongues is mysterious; the person speaking the language cannot understand and must rely on Holy Spirit.

It is no accident that the Holy Spirit needs to join with our spirit to affirm that we are His children (Romans 8:16). We cannot even speak the language of heaven that brings the affirmation without this divine connection.

The gift of tongues, or spirit language, then, is a gift that transports our natural ability to speak on a supernatural level. With the gift of tongues, we as sons and daughters of heaven can speak what heaven speaks.

Through our spirit to Holy Spirit, *pneuma-to-Pneuma* connection, we are strengthened both in the affirmation of our new position and the realization of our new potential. And we are fortified to such a degree that we can now realize the full power of the armor of God.

Without the strength that comes directly from the spiritual gift of tongues, the armor of God is more a theological pursuit with no real effect on our lives. To be a person of truth, righteousness, and peace, to be a person of faith without spiritual strength is flat out exhausting. At the end of the day, it is also impossible. I know. I have tried.

Trying to do super in my natural strength has caused me to almost give up altogether. Paul knows this, that's why he bookends the inventory of spiritual armor we are to possess and utilize with yet another admonishment to tap into the gift of praying in the Spirit in verse 18,

"And pray in the Spirit on all occasions with all kinds of prayers and requests."

It makes perfect tactical sense for the enemy to keep us from this gift. You see, the gift of tongues strengthens our awareness of our identity, strengthens our spiritual capacity, and empowers our spiritual arsenal. The gift of tongues joins the super to the natural and releases us to live a totally new kind of normal.

Strengthened to Win

Years ago my mum came across a very old violin in her back shed. It was one that her mother had used, but it was in a sad state of disrepair. Our daughter Jessie was learning violin at the time, and so my mum gave it to her to get repaired so it could be played once again.

As a musician, I know a bit about instruments and what causes resonance. I even know when something is in pitch or out of pitch. I also know how to use tools to build and make things. However, this precious instrument was well beyond my ability to restore. It needed to go to a violinmaker.

We found a German violinmaker, who worked in a small workshop in a neighboring suburb outside of the city of Melbourne, Australia. When we walked in, we saw violins at all stages of production on his workbench. We saw tools used for making violins—apparatuses the likes of which we had never seen before. This violinmaker knew how a violin is constructed, and what was needed to repair, restore, or even reconstruct it. He knew how to get the best sound out of such an instrument.

God is the human maker. As we saw earlier in Genesis 1, we are made in His image. And as 1 Chronicles 16:34 informs us,

"Give thanks to the Lord, for he is good! His faithful love endures forever."

If God is always good and loving, and He alone is the human maker, then it stands to reason His gifts are good, adequate, and necessary, and are to be used in a loving manner. If God is the good, loving, human maker, and He has given good gifts to make us strong, then it also stands to reason that we should access those gifts to become all that He intends for us to become in order to walk in the fullness of His goodness.

The spiritual gift of tongues is one of the tools that God gives us to access spiritual strength, so we are empowered to strengthen the body of Christ and do even greater works than those of Jesus.

The gift of tongues strengthens us by bringing our hearts in harmony with the will of God. In Romans 8:16 and Romans 26-27 we have seen that our spirit is connected to the Holy Spirit. And so when He calls us to pray in tongues, we are praying in unity with His Spirit and in harmony with the will of God. This act is a vital step in the process of living a totally new kind of normal. Through the gift of tongues, God has given us the super to enable the natural and strengthen us to overcome the opposing forces of our adversary.

Think again for a moment about an army. If just one member of the army is strong and the rest are weak, will they have the ability to win battles? What if two or three are strong? No. It is the desire and will of the captain to ensure that all members are strong and ready to advance the battle forward to win.

Remember it is the goal of our enemy to make us spiritually weak by cutting off supply lines and then dividing and conquering. But when we operate in the gift of tongues we draw on that language which *God* has given to help sustain and strengthen us.

It's for Everyone

My wife Julie and I are two very different people. Our differences go way beyond our differences in gender. We are not better or worse. Just different.

Julie is a feeler; I am a doer. Julie cries at the drop of a hat, while my tear ducts regularly experience long seasons of drought. Julie is very detailed oriented. I am made for the big picture. Julie is emotionally recharged through alone time; I need people. Lots and lots of people!

Even though we both have more differences than there is time or space to write, we both operate with the gifts that God designed to strengthen us. The really great thing is that we use these strengthening gifts in ways that make sense to who we are designed to be.

When God made you, He broke the mold! It is a scientific and statistical fact that there can never be another you. God is creative beyond compare—look around! He made introverts and extroverts. God made those of you who love variety more than routine and vice-versa. Some work better alone, some in a team. In the same way, the personality differences of Bible characters are extreme: Peter was a *go-getter*, Jeremiah, *melancholy*. John was a *feeler*, Paul was very *task oriented*. There are no right or wrong personalities. And that means there are no right or wrong personalities for the strengthening gift of tongues; otherwise God would be saying, "I only want some of you to be strong."

And we know enough about His good character and nature to know that God would never make such a statement.

The gift of tongues is for everyone!

Christmas Lights

I hate Christmas lights! There. I have said it. I can fix and repair pretty complex electrical equipment and machinery. But Christmas lights? They are the bane of my existence. They are humiliating to intelligent beings. I reckon they were a plan of the enemy from the beginning of time to keep men perpetually frustrated during a season of thankfulness...

One year, in late November, I was confronted with the annual question that plagues me every Christmas, "Do I just throw all of last year's lights in the trash and buy new ones, or do I dare take them on, and believe that this year will somehow be different?"

I decided to walk the edge of insanity and tackle the lights I already had. While I am no Clarke Griswold, our lights look pretty nice when they are all up. Most of them were positioned in place when I turned them on. With virtually no surprise to me, there was the strand that worked, the strands that were on, then off, then on, then... off, on, off. And there was *that one* light strand that looked as though it would not know an electron if it bit on the bulb!

I am not sure just how long I attempted to repair that one strand, it felt like years. I took every last bulb out of the very long strand of lights and tested it individually. I even went to the extreme of taking the little holder off the bottom of each of the bulbs, all three-hundred of them, to make sure the connections to the bulb base was clean. Still nothing!

I was reduced to complete helplessness. Frustrated would be an understatement.

It was my young son who found the very complex solution to my mind-altering problem. Holding the end of the strand up in his right hand he yelled,

"Dad, it looks like you haven't plugged them in!"

From my experience as a pastor for many years now, it is my observation that the body of Christ is spending a lot of time tinkering with the lights, trying every last thing conceivable to be the light of the world. The church seems to seek complex answers in lieu of a very simple solution. And the church wonders why things don't work the way they have been promised they should. For the most part, it isn't plugged into the power source made available to it.

The Holy Spirit is the power source. And we need to plug in. Tongues is one of the ways we plug in.

Because tongues isn't something to be understood, many have suggested that it involves unplugging our minds. Nothing could be further from the truth. The gift of tongues doesn't unplug our mind. The gift of tongues plugs the mind in to a totally new revelation of God's power.

Paul makes this concept very practical,

"Therefore, I urge you, brothers and sisters, in view of God's mercy, to offer your bodies as a living sacrifice, holy and pleasing to God—this is your true and proper worship. Do not conform to the pattern of this world, but be transformed by the renewing of your mind. Then you will be able to test and approve what God's will is—his good, pleasing and perfect will" (Romans 12:1-2).

The word *present* is the Greek word *paristēmi*. It means to *bring near and place at the disposal of another*. Paul calls for a decisive commitment to fully surrender our whole body and mind to God.

Verse 2 tells us how we can maintain that commitment by renewing our mind and not following the fashion and pattern of the world.

The word *renew* comes from the Greek word *anakainōsis* and means to *renovate and change completely for the better*. The word does not carry even the slightest connotation that the process of mind renewal and renovation involves "unplugging our minds" in any way. If anything, renewing our minds suggests full engagement of our minds in the process of total renovation. Can you imagine renovating a house without the house even coming into contact with the work? Such an idea is nonsensical.

How I Received the Gift of Tongues

Even with all this in mind, stepping into the use of the gift of tongues was scary for me. As I have mentioned previously, I was a Cessationist for the first 10 years of my ministry. But thankfully, God in His goodness provided a person I could trust, a friend named Bill, to help step me through. God did this because He wanted me to have access to the super to go with my natural. He wanted to restore me to His original intent, to be a Releaser in deep communion with Him as a son, to speak how heaven speaks and live a totally new kind of normal.

While there are many ways to receive the gift of tongues I want to demystify the process by explaining how this process worked for me.

I needed to trust God with my mind. Sounds basic enough. Oddly, while I found it very easy to trust God with other areas of my life, it was much harder to give Him my mind. While I said out loud that God was my God, in practice my mind was. If there were ever questions of faith verses rationale, the mind would win the day every time.

So, *my* first step was to trust that my good God, the human maker and giver of my mind, was trustworthy enough for me to give my mind back, to surrender it to Him for full renewal and renovation. Make Him my God.

As an act of submission of my mind to God, I allowed Bill to ask me a series of questions that demanded honest answers. Answers that were consistent with who my mind espoused and trusted God to be. And so the questions began.

"Is God a good God and did He make you?" Bill asked.

"Yes"

"Does He speak to you?"

"Yes."

"Does He give good gifts to make you strong?"

"Yes, I believe He does."

"If you asked Him for one good thing that He said you could have;

would He give you something different?"

"No"

"If you trust He made you and speaks to you, is good, and that He gives good gifts. If you believe in your mind that He would give you a good thing that He said you could have if you asked Him. Do you trust Him to give you a good word, a word you don't understand in the natural, to get your heavenly prayer language started so that you can begin to walk in the fullness of strength He has for you?"

"Yes, I believe I can trust Him with that." I said.

"So ask Him for a word. And trust Him that the first word that comes to your mind after praying for that word."

Even though I hold a theological degree, my prayer was as basic as that of a young child speaking to his dad. It went something like this,

"Dear God, I know you are good. I know you speak to me. I know you have good gifts for me to enjoy and to make me as strong as You have designed me to be. I now trust You, that the gift of tongues is one of those gifts. I confess I have been trying to do things in a strength that is limited to what my mind allows. So I ask that You give me this good gift. I ask that You now give me a word to get started. I trust that this word is from You, even though my mind doesn't understand it. In Jesus' name. Amen."

Bills questions were based on sound Scripture. Scriptures I knew but had never really *known,*

"Ask and it will be given to you; seek and you will find; knock and the door will be opened to you. For everyone who asks receives; the one who seeks finds; and to the one who knocks, the door will be opened. Which of you, if your son asks for bread, will give him a stone? Or if he asks for a fish, will give him a snake? If you, then, though you are evil, know how to give good gifts to your children, how much more will your Father in heaven give good gifts to those who ask him! So in everything, do to others what you would have them do to you, for this sums up the Law and the Prophets." (Matthew 7:7-12).

The word came. The word, I trusted was from God. My mind didn't understand the meaning of the word, but I did know that it was a word from God, because it came with sound reasoning and peace. And while our enemy can counterfeit many things, he cannot counterfeit peace. That single word became the foundation word, upon which a new heavenly language was constructed; a word that accelerated the process of renewal and renovation of my mind.

Bill encouraged me to spend a short amount of time each day praying that word over several times. A couple of weeks into it, a second word came. Then a few days later, a third. Then what seemed like a sentence shortly after that. New lilts and tones, inflections and sounds began to emerge from my heart. I could feel the tide of my spirit rise in ways I had *never* experienced before. My heavenly language emerged, one word at a time, in the way a young child learns a new language, one word at a time.

My mind never checked out. It became increasingly plugged in. My mind engaged in my prayer life more than ever as pictures, visions, and revelation would come while praying in my new heavenly language. I saw things I had not encountered since those first days of coming into a relationship with Jesus at the youth camp many years before. I didn't ever know my mind had such a capacity to see and understand spiritual things like this. I could *feel* my spirit connect with God's Spirit. The spiritual connection became a physical thing.

I have found that this gift of tongues has joined God's super to my natural. When I am down, I can feel my inner spiritual strength increase—and quickly. I see previously immovable spiritual forces shifting before my eyes. I see why my adversary has kept me away from this strengthening gift for so long. Now, God is transforming me, renovating me into a spiritual force to be reckoned with!

Heart, Soul, and Mind

In western culture, intellect has become God. It's called humanism and it is all about what seems right to a man.

You will not see a rising measure of supernatural strength and change by keeping some parts conformed to the values system of this world. He who has lordship over the mind *owns* the person. Have you given God lordship over your mind? Or does your mind still own you?

If you're serious about surrendering fully to Christ, if you want your personal life, family life, and business life to be all that you know God has planned for it, then I encourage you to give Him your whole being, heart, soul, and mind (Matt 22:37) and be transformed, renewed, and renovated.

Just recently I heard Bill Johnson say, *"I cannot afford to even think a thought about me that God doesn't have about me."*

Heaven's thoughts about me are way bigger than what my natural, puny mind thinks about me. The gift of tongues is increasing my awareness of who I am as a son, because greater increase in revelation about my own identity is coming to my mind from Him.

The gift of tongues is not about *unplugging* our minds. It's about plugging our minds *in* to the conversations of heaven!

I Have Been Looking for a Chance to Give Them to You...

My dad left a series of messages on my home phone when I was first married. I was so busy that, to my embarrassment, I never listened to them or returned his calls. We lived sixteen-hundred miles from him and a good period of time passed. Then my mum got word to me that dad was unwell.

We made a trip back to visit him and while with him one day, he beckoned my mum toward his wallet sitting on the chair near his bed. He pulled out some money and said, "You probably don't remember, Mark, but I mentioned long before you got married that when that day came I would give you some funds to help out. I know it's not much, but this belongs to you. I left you some messages on the phone some time ago, but you never got back to me. I have been looking for a chance to give them to you."

There are gifts of the Holy Spirit that our heavenly Father has given to His children that are designed for the expressed purpose of taking their natural and make it *super*. To a restored person with Jesus residing within, these supernatural gifts provide so much spiritual strength that he or she is able to move situations, atmospheres, and circumstances against these opposing spiritually resistive forces. These gifts make it possible to establish the Kingdom of God on the earth and live a totally new kind of normal.

The gift of tongues is one of those gifts. The gift of tongues will allow God to work through your mind in new ways to renew and renovate your personal life, your family life, and your business. It is yours to access. You are invited to speak the language of heaven. Perhaps God has been calling, leaving messages on your heart for you to get back to Him, looking for a chance to give you a good gift.

I encourage you to receive this very good gift today.

9

Surfers and Tsunamis

*"Sometimes, when you have spent a long time rejecting the gifts
of the Spirit and come to believe in them, you almost feel as if you
are being born again. You feel as if you have a whole new Bible...
Things that you had relegated to the first century now become a
possibility for today's church."*

—Jack Deere

You Are That Surfer

The sun rises at an ungodly hour on the days surrounding the summer solstice on Queensland's Gold Coast. Just fifty miles north of the eastern cardinal point of the Australian mainland, this is a place where you can see the sun raise its head around 4:40 AM.

Living on the Gold Coast at that time of the year was *painful* for a family with two kids aged three and under. With the astro-twilight kicking in around 3:10 AM, it was not unusual to hear the kids begin to stir by 4:00 AM. An early riser, I would often dress the kids, put them in the car, and drive ten minutes to the beach. I would walk them in the stroller and watch the sun fully rise. It was my gift to my not-so-early-rising wife.

By the time Julie was pregnant with child number three, the predawn beach walk became routine. One morning the routine was interrupted by the strangest of things.

We arrived at the beach, along with the usual runners, lifeguards, surfers, and other sleepy looking dads with wide awake kids, all ready for our morning *greeting* from Mr. Sun. We went for our standard hour-long walk, kids in the stroller. But as I was preparing to put them back in the car and head home to make breakfast, someone spoke to me by name.

"Mark, I want you to buckle the kids in the car, and go back and look at the water."

It was unusual, for two reasons. First, it was a strange request. Second, there was no one around. I turned to see who it was. The nearest person was fifty yards away. Shaking my head, I turned back toward the inside of the car, and immediately heard it again,

"Mark, I want you to buckle the kids in the car, and go back and look at the water."

Feeling a bit like a confused Samuel, I pushed for a third time, and, sure enough, same voice, same words. I began performing a rapid-fire mental inventory of my own psychological well-being. Was I over-stressed? Overworked? Overweight? Over sleepy? Nope. Had I eaten poorly? Exposed myself to sick people or let myself get run down? None of those either.

In those days, believing God spoke to me, apart from His Word, was a thought I was not prepared to entertain. So, this was indeed a peculiar experience, one that caused me to question my own sanity. I checked my pulse to see if my heart rate was racing and read a nearby sign to make sure I was still *with it*. Everything checked out fine.

I decided that I had nothing to lose, and that no one would be harmed. I did as the *mystery voice* had requested. Looking to my left and right to make sure this was not some sort of *set up*, I proceeded to walk the short distance to the top of the bluff where I was parked and then looked at the water as *instructed*.

There was nothing that seemed out of place or worthy of such a peculiar experience, just the usual unremarkable group of Grommets, young teen surfers who surfed before school. A couple of surf lifesaving boats were doing their morning drills, and a handful of distant joggers faded into the surf's haze.

I was about to turn back to the car of restless kids when something *did* capture my attention. A professional looking surfer emerged out of his Volkswagon van. With his tri-fin surfboard tucked under his arm, his shaggy sun-bleached hair blowing about his head, and leg-rope velcroed to his ankle, he trotted up to water's edge and, throwing his board before him, he dove belly first onto it and began to paddle out.

He captured my attention for one main reason: there was no surf that morning worthy enough to entice that caliber of surfer to get out of bed. Did *he* have kids strapped in the car as well? Or . . . did he know something I did not?

I stayed and watched.

He paddled for several minutes until he was a few hundred yards out from the edge of the beach. And he sat. He looked around then lay back down and paddled left for ten seconds. He sat again. Looking some more, he paddled out further, ten or so seconds, before sitting again. This pattern continued for several minutes.

And then I saw it.

A giant seven-to-eight foot set, like glass, began to form and roll in. In the local vernacular, this was the famous "Burleigh Barrel." Burleigh Heads is a suburban beach in southeast Queensland that attracts professional surfers from all around the world, and the Burleigh Barrel is the famous break that draws them.

As the Burleigh Barrel drew close, *my* man began to paddle at just the right speed to catch it at its perfect crest and peak power. And, boy oh boy, did he own that wave! He flew at an amazing speed down the wave's glassy white-veined face as the barrel began to form. He entered the barrel, knees bent. Then with his left arm outstretched behind him, his fingers stroked the inner wall of the wave. The spray danced from his fingertips like musical notes on a page.

As the barrel began to close out, my surfer appeared still crouched, and then he stood straight up. With what looked like a single snap of his left leg, he pointed the nose of his board toward the back of the wave and effortlessly launched himself clear off the top with his arms in a victory position over his head. Then, collecting his board, he proceeded to paddle back to shore. That was all he came for.

I stood there. Frozen. Amazed. I was completely astonished at the spectacle I had just witnessed. I watched as he high-fived the starry-eyed Grommets on the shore who had also seen the display of surfing prowess.

As the surfer hit the beachside shower, I turned back to the car, thankful that I had listened and followed the instruction of whatever it was that had directed me just minutes before. Then I heard *mystery voice* again. This time it came with a new sense of authority.

"Mark, you are that surfer!"

So clear and loud was the voice that this time I responded out loud.

"What? What do you mean?" I hesitantly asked.

"I am going to teach you how to catch *my* waves, the waves that no one else can see. And you will show others how to catch them as well. There is a spiritual tsunami coming. Get ready. Get people ready."

So exactly *how* do you tell your wife about such a weird experience?

Not a single textbook that I had read during my theological training up to that point had prepared me for communicating an event like this.

"Sweetheart, you need to wake up. Something *really* weird just happened."

Listening intently, and asking appropriate questions, she eventually concluded,

"That *is really* weird!"

I agreed, and for the next twelve years, we would never speak of that moment again.

The Gift of Prophecy

The gift of prophecy is the second gift of the Holy Spirit that strengthens the sons and daughters of heaven by joining God's super to their natural. It does so by granting the son or daughter of heaven the ability to speak how heaven speaks. Just like the gift of tongues, the gift of prophecy is designed to provide spiritual strength, strength which empowers believers to move situations, atmospheres, and circumstances against the spiritually resistive forces that oppose the Kingdom of God on the earth.

In the hands of God's Kingdom Releasers, the gift of prophecy can build up, fuel up, and mobilize the people of God to boldly move into miracle territory. Miracle territory is that place where natural people, under the authority of God, with the power of the Holy Spirit, can pull heaven to earth and make *all things possible* in otherwise impossible situations.

Just like the gift of tongues, the gift of prophecy has a corporate and an individual application. *Unlike* tongues, however, the gift of prophecy is also an office or five-fold gift. We see this in Ephesians 4:11-13,

"So Christ himself gave the apostles, the prophets, the evangelists, the pastors and teachers, to equip his people for works of service, so that the body of Christ may be built up until we all reach unity in the faith and in the knowledge of the Son of God and become mature, attaining to the whole measure of the fullness of Christ."(NIV).

This five-fold gift of prophecy is different to the individual gift of prophecy as seen in 1 Corinthians 14:31,

"For you can all prophesy in turn so that everyone may be instructed and encouraged."(NIV).

In this chapter, I will focus on the individual gift of prophecy.

The Journey of More

Recently, while journaling with my daughter, Alex-Anne, early one morning, I caught a glimpse of the transformation in my thinking regarding the gifts of the Holy Spirit. For a large part of my early Christian life, I actively and purposely moved away from the gifts. I encouraged people to do likewise. In those early years, the gifts seemed weird and fake, and I failed to understand their purpose.

While journaling through Acts 8:29-31, I realized how different my thinking has become.

Here is my journal entry:

Title: To Walk or Run

S: "*The Holy Spirit said to Philip, "Go over and walk along beside the carriage." Philip ran over and heard the man reading from the prophet Isaiah. Philip asked, "Do you understand what you are reading?" The man replied, "How can I, unless someone instructs me?" And he urged Philip to come up into the carriage and sit with him.*"

O: When God said *walk*, Philip ran! He was so expectant for the workings of God that he did not, could not, delay. How could he walk when confronted with an opportunity like this? He had a chance to step back into miracle territory! He wasn't to be disappointed. The Ethiopian eunuch, at *just the right time*, was reading something he needed help interpreting. God goes before Philip and prepares the way for Philip to host an encounter.

A: Do I run with expectancy or walk in hesitation? When God says, "Go," I want to be the one who is leading the charge and *running* toward, leading others, facilitating an encounter with God.

P: Father, I want to hear Your voice every day! Show me where to go, using any means You want, and please show me what to do when I get there. I am excited to see You at work and expectant that You will fulfill Your purposes by revealing Yourself to others through me.

Amen.

That journal entry revealed a shift in my thinking. There was a great difference between that young father who sixteen years earlier thought he was going crazy when a *mystery voice* spoke to him about looking at water and the somewhat older dad writing that journal.

While the experience of hearing God's voice was immediate, the shift in my understanding to speak what heaven was speaking occurred gradually. Transformation takes time. I had taken years to read, think, question, and observe the Christian experience to which I was exposed.

That encounter on the beach along with others birthed an inner yearning for a greater God encounter. I had tasted His presence, and I had heard Him speak, and I felt like there was so much more. I wanted to hear His voice like Philip had.

I didn't feel like I could tell my mature clergy friends. They too were Cessationist, and I feared they would think I was losing it, so I journeyed quietly.

I was on the journey to become a full-time pastor. And this yearning for more was producing some new questions and leading to some new conclusions about God and me. I began to determine that if Christianity was merely reduced to an irreducible minimum, a set of rules and regulations surrounding some cool songs, a three-point sermon, some announcements, lots of meetings, and a nebulous historical figure, then I may as well have just stayed in the Navy.

Then God introduced and used a man named Rob to lead me to the place where I began to *eagerly desire* the *more* of God.

esley's Quadrilateral, and Prophecy

Rob was a pastor of a nearby church who was generous with his time. He would meet with me every couple of months to answer my newfound questions regarding the experiences of God. Rob wasn't a theological weirdo. He was grounded, a man of integrity. I felt I could trust him.

Rob spoke of daily encounters with God, encounters that caused my heart to leap. Encounters that revealed to me that he knew how to speak the language of heaven. I longed for these encounters to be true in my own experience. And Rob wasn't disconnected from the real world. I found his understanding about how the narrative of God was playing out through history revelatory.

Rob dared to ask me fresh questions about the nature and character of God. Honest questions that caused my conscience to prick. I began to realize there was a major inconsistency in my own hermeneutic regarding God's nature and character versus my understanding of how He wanted to relate to me.

Without realizing it, I was using a process I later came to know as the Wesleyan Quadrilateral to make a significant shift in my thinking. The Wesleyan Quadrilateral is a framework of assessment that revivalist John Wesley articulated to explain how he determined truth. In essence, Wesley's Quadrilateral compares and contrasts Scripture, tradition, reason, and experience to arrive at truth determination. It is a powerful metric because it engages many elements of our humanity in the process. My will, my conscience, and my heart, as well as my mind, were arriving at places of new trust with God's character and nature and were increasingly at peace with new revelation pertaining to my identity.

The shift in my thinking pertaining to the gift of prophecy began to take place around this same time. I could feel myself arriving at a place of peace in my understanding of God's nature and character that helped me to see old information in a new light. It was an experience not unlike watching a kid's movie when you are ten years old, then watching it again as an adult and realizing there were layers of humor embedded in the storyline that was there all along but you had previously missed. My new and growing understanding of the gift of prophecy was fast becoming a catalyst for allowing God to work through me.

As I examined Scriptures from which I had previously drawn conclusions, I began to see that the Holy Spirit gift of prophecy, since Pentecost, has been a third form of the prophetic work of God. The first two forms being, infallible Old Testament prophecy and infallible New Testament prophetic writing. I came to realize Scripture was revealing this third form of the prophetic utterance as a Holy Spirit gift. And this language of heaven was still available to me today.

With time carefully taken to recalibrate my hermeneutic, my Scriptural, traditional, experiential, and reasoned conclusions, I understood the revelation that the third form of the prophetic word comes spontaneously after a person with the gift of prophecy has an encounter with Holy Spirit. This gift is available to everyone who seeks it and is often mixed with a person's own experiences. I also saw how, given the third form of the gift of prophecy doesn't carry the same authoritative weight as the first two forms of the gift, it can at times be incorrect.

I have since also observed that prophecy, putting the language of heaven in the hands of fallible people, is not problematic. God in His goodness has provided the gift of words of spiritual wisdom, as well as His written Word as tools to be used to help assess the accuracy of this new prophetic word. Some of these themes are captured in 1 Corinthians 14:32, 1 Corinthians 14:3, and 1 Corinthians 4:29 respectively,

"Remember that people who prophesy are in control of their spirit and can take turns . . . But one who prophesies strengthens others, encourages them, and comforts them . . . Let two or three people prophesy, and let the others evaluate what is said."

The release of the Holy Spirit gift of prophecy will always serve the Kingdom purpose of building up, fueling up, and mobilizing the people of God to boldly move into miracle territory,

"... if the bugler doesn't sound a clear call, how will the soldiers know they are being called to battle?" (1 Corinthians 14:8).

The battle described in Ephesians 6:12 is a supernatural one,

"For we are not fighting against flesh-and-blood enemies, but against evil rulers and authorities of the unseen world, against mighty powers in this dark world, and against evil spirits in the heavenly places."

It is a battle that requires us to walk in miracle territory. Fighting supernatural resistive forces with natural means is ineffective. Only through joining God's super to our natural can we move situations, atmospheres, and circumstances against the spiritually resistive forces.

The gift of prophecy will *always* call us to walk in miracle territory because miracle territory is where the battle is. It is also where the encounter with God awaits.

Miracle Territory—Decreasers, Policers, and Releasers

We are all called to live in miracle territory. We are all designed to experience His super in our natural. The reality is, *Decreasers* don't believe in miracle territory and *Policers* are afraid of it. Such rejection of the miraculous has resulted in the larger part of the body of Christ either discounting the Holy Spirit gift of prophecy or finding themselves unable to trust God enough to access and utilize it.

Releasers, on the other hand, live in such a way that miracle territory is a part of their everyday lives.

Do you live as a *Releaser* in miracle territory in your personal, family, and business life? Or are you stuck as a *Decreaser* or *Policer* in the natural land of predictability and control? Take a minute to reflect and ask Holy Spirit to give you truth as you ask these following questions:

Six Signs of a Decreaser Paradigm

1. As a son or daughter of heaven who has Jesus living in you, do you make personal, business, or family life decisions based purely on empirical evidence and personal desire?

2. Is your desire for business success more about your profile and press than God's presence and power being displayed?

3. Are you always looking to *figure out* the problem, issue, or concern before taking action?

4. Do your views of where God is leading you change with your emotions?

5. Is your purpose defined more by how well you achieve goals than the Kingdom goals of walking in the fullness of the image of God, of being a spiritual mentor to your family, of seeing a generation get the encounter with God they were created for?

6. Do your actions demonstrate that you *practically* do not believe God has an opinion when it comes to what you decide and how you live?

If you answered *yes* to many or all of these questions, you are seeing the signs and symptoms of a Decreaser paradigm.

Six Signs of a Policer Paradigm

1. As a son or daughter of heaven who has Jesus living in you, when you identify the types of decisions that *need* to be made in your personal, business, and family life, do you see the gap between your capacity to steward the decision and the implications of such decisions? Does that realization cause you to retreat and legislate logical, natural behavior to produce a lesser outcome?

2. Is your desire for security based more on bottom lines, ROIs (return on investments), KPIs (key performance indicators), and solid network relationships than your identity as a son or daughter of heaven?

3. Are you justifying determining the allocation of your resources, personal and/or business, toward philanthropic and humanitarian enterprise more from a place of what you can get out of it, than from a desire to see people genuinely come into an eternity changing relationship encounter with God?

4. Is your assessment of success based more on ROIs and KPIs than relationships that are infused with love?

5. Do you conclude that goals attained through control-based decisions are evidence of God's affirmation?

6. Do you assess the positive responses of your peers regarding your controlled outcomes as affirmation from God that you are walking in His presence?

If you find you are answering *yes* to many or all of these questions, then you are seeing the signs and symptoms of a Policer paradigm.

Six Signs of a Releaser Paradigm

1. As a son or daughter of heaven, who has Jesus living in you, do you see the types of decisions that need to be made in your personal,

business, or family life, and with a sense of expectancy and a rising tide of faith, inspire those around you to take hold of another opportunity to trust God in new ways?

2. Do you find dissatisfaction in your spirit when you find a pattern of controlled and predictable outcomes emerging in your personal, family, or business life?

3. When a person shares their dream or vision with you, do you feel a rise in your own creativity and desire to find a way to help them?

4. Do you see time with people, whether at home, work or play, as an opportunity for a deeper encounter with God through love?

5. Are you excited to see how your leadership can help other Kingdom people fulfill their calling?

6. Do you feel uninspired when you have more answers than questions?

If you answered *yes* to many or all of these questions, then you are seeing the signs and symptoms of a Releaser paradigm.

The Releaser paradigm is the only one that will cause you to consistently walk in miracle territory. You have no need for God's super to meet your natural unless you are walking in miracle territory. These Releaser questions reveal if you find greater security in controlled outcomes or if you find greater security through intimacy with a heavenly Father of always perfect love.

Watchman Nee, in his classic, *The Normal Christian Life*, put it this way,

> "We all have the same Christ dwelling within, but revelation of some new need will lead us spontaneously to trust Him to live out His life in that particular."

Releasers live in an upside down world. Releasers' security is determined by proximity to their heavenly Father's heart. Proximity to His heart calls out identity as a son or daughter of heaven, and proximity to His heart is most clearly experienced in miracle territory—because that's where the battle is. That's where God is.

God longs for His super to meet our natural. Miracle territory is the place where that happens.

Tell Daryl He Has the Gift of Writing...

Since that time on the beach where God spoke to me, I have been discovering through Scripture, tradition, reason, and experience, that God was calling me to become a Releaser of the conversations of heaven—to speak how heaven speaks. Over the years that followed, I grew increasingly dissatisfied with the false sense of security that the world, and even the church, offered me.

I could feel the shift in my spirit away from the paradigm of Policer. My attitude toward the Holy Spirit gift of prophecy was moving from weird to wonder. I grew in my desire to experience the Holy Spirit gift of prophecy. I sensed Holy Spirit calling me, *pneuma* to *Pneuma*, deeper in to miracle territory, deeper in to an encounter with my heavenly Father's heart, until finally, I was ready to partner with God, I was willing to use prophecy in a powerfully revelatory way.

I was at a leadership training event in Hawaii in April 2008. Incidentally, Jesus speaks *really* clear in places like Hawaii! It had taken around five years, but I was finally at a place where I had developed an increasing comfort level being surrounded with people who both desired and experienced greater encounters with God.

One morning I was eating breakfast with nine other delegates when my gaze met one of the group named Daryl. In that moment, I heard it again. The *mystery voice*. That same one that had invited me to look at water so many years earlier. The voice that spoke of surfers and tsunamis. That same voice spoke on the island of Oahu. No surprise, it got my attention.

"Tell Daryl he has the gift of writing."

This time my response was more of a mumble under my breath than an audible dialogue with *mystery voice*.

"I can't say that. I don't know him from Adam!" I muttered.

But just like the first time, the *mystery voice* was persistent!

"Tell Daryl he has the gift of writing."

I clued in a bit quicker to this supernatural game. I yielded after just two rounds. I felt I was on safe ground given that this group of people were considerably more used to strangers saying weird things to them.

Carefully, sweaty palmed, and a stammering a little, I looked back at Daryl and said,

"Daryl."

"Yes. What's up?" He asked.

"I believe God . . ." (I said God, because one thing Rob had taught me well, is that when it *is* God speaking, it will always encourage, and even though what I was about to share was simple, it *was* at least encouraging.) ". . . is wanting to encourage you by declaring you have a gift of writing sitting inside of you."

There. I said it. It was off my chest. Now my palms could go back to room temperature.

Not really knowing how someone responds in situations like these, I was relieved to hear Darryl reply with,

"Thanks, Mark, I receive that."

In a moment of pride and relief we Aussie's will say, "I feel pretty *chuffed* with myself." I didn't say it but I could have.

Figuring that was it, I went about my day—breakout sessions, small group meetings, and some down time. Everything was going according to the schedule. Then Daryl came *running* in. Yes, *running*! A rather strong lad, he picked me up and bear hugged me hard enough to nearly shake Jesus out of me.

"What's going on, mate?" I gasped.

"After that word you gave, I went back to my room and rang my wife. I did that because unknown to you, she is a writer."

"Okay," I said with a nervous expectancy.

"She had said to me many years ago that she felt that I, too, had a gift of writing. I told her that I would see it as a confirmation from God if one day a complete stranger comes up to me and declares that I have a gift of writing!"

Now I was just about hugging Jesus out of Daryl! Tears, joy, laughter, back slapping. But more, way more importantly—I had stepped into miracle territory, and I encountered God there! The power of the prophetic encounter with God changed our lives forever that day because the conversation of heaven over Daryl had been released. And not just our lives were changed that day, anyone who reads Daryl's words will be impacted by the gift of prophecy.

Tongues and Prophecy—Connecting His Super to Our Natural

Let's take a deeper look at the strengthening gift of prophecy. In 1 Corinthians 14:1 we read,

"Let love be your highest goal! But you should also desire the special abilities the Spirit gives—especially the ability to prophesy."

Paul uses the Greek word *mallon*, meaning, *to a much greater degree*, to describe the kind of intention we should have concerning prophecy. Why?

I believe the answer lies in the following verses 2-4,

"For if you have the ability to speak in tongues, you will be talking only to God, since people won't be able to understand you. You will be speaking by the power of the Spirit, but it will all be mysterious. But one who prophesies strengthens others, encourages them, and comforts them.

A person who speaks in tongues is strengthened personally, but one who speaks a word of prophecy strengthens the entire church."

The metaphor of the human body is helpful in determining the functional difference between the two strengthening gifts of tongues and prophecy that connect God's super to our natural.

The gift of tongues is like a right arm strengthening itself with a dumbbell. It is good and appropriate for right arms to use dumbbells to strengthen themselves. Dumbbells are made for the expressed purpose of strengthening arms. But while the right arm will be strengthened using the dumbbell, the right arm is serving no purpose in strengthening, say, the left leg.

The gift of prophecy is a supernatural strengthening gift of the Holy Spirit that enables a "right arm" body member to strengthen a "left leg" body member. It accomplishes this task by releasing the presence of Kingdom power through heaven's words. It unlocks potential and releases vision, building up, fueling, and mobilizing a person in readiness for the journey into miracle territory. It's a supernatural invitation because the battle is a supernatural one. It was Darryl knowing beyond a shadow of a doubt in his innermost being that God wanted him to enter the battle by taking a risk to write.

The word *ekklesia*, used in 1 Corinthians 14:4 by Paul means, *"the whole body of Christians scattered throughout the earth"* Given the opportunity, God, through the gift of prophecy, will mobilize a Kingdom army!

The Metrics of Prophecy

The metric of an individual prophetic word being from God is simple. It's spelled out in 1 Corinthians 14:4.

Edify, which means to build faith in others.

Encouragement, which means to be a positive spiritual influence on another person.

Comfort, which carries the connotation of releasing the presence of God over the life of another person.

Prophecy is not meant to be some type of doomsday language. There is no place for manipulation, control, or fear with the use of the Holy Spirit gift of prophecy. If the prophetic word is one that is from God, then it should always be consistent with God's written Word and the person of Jesus. It should bear witness to the claims of Jesus and resonate with Holy Spirit within you.

John puts this perfectly in Revelation 19:10,

"Worship only God. For the essence of prophecy is to give a clear witness for Jesus."

The Greek word for essence is, *martyria*. This word is a legal term meaning, *judicial evidence*. There is a legal decree released from God through the prophetic word that is consistent with God's character and nature. Actuated by the works of Jesus' life, death, and resurrection, the gift of prophecy calls out the true identity in His sons and daughters throughout His body, building them up, encouraging them and bringing His comfort to ground zero of their specific need.

The Holy Spirit gift of prophecy releases the language of heaven over a person or situation. It is the current commentary of heaven over a current activity. It will draw a person closer to God, not push them away. The Holy Spirit gift of prophecy is speaking how heaven speaks.

There is an endless amount of information flying through the airwaves every moment of every day. If you have a television or radio you can tune it in to the corresponding signal. God is talking *all the time*. He has opinion and commentary, wisdom and revelation for everyone, every day, for every situation. The gift of the Holy Spirit, known as the gift of prophecy, tunes our hearts toward Him to receive what He is currently saying and then pass it on to others.

What languages does God use to speak? Bible, pictures, dreams, numbers, colors, visions—all of His creation. Paul describes this in his book written to the Roman Church 1:20,

> *"For ever since the world was created, people have seen the earth and sky. Through everything God made, they can clearly see his invisible qualities—his eternal power and divine nature. So they have no excuse for not knowing God."*

The prophetic word of God calls our attention to where our heavenly Father's heart is currently focused, and what His heart is currently focused on. I discovered that day in Hawaii that the more I desired what my heavenly Father desires, the louder the prophetic voice of God becomes and the more time I spend in miracle territory.

God has placed the Holy Spirit gift of prophecy into the hands of His Kingdom Releasers. He has given the gift of prophecy to build up, fuel up, and mobilize the people of God to boldly move into miracle territory. The enemy has kept it from us long enough. It is time we take hold of this powerful gift.

Calling All Surfers

The place was Bethel church in Redding, California, and the event was a Leadership Conference. It was an unremarkable Thursday in November. The year was 2011.

A prophetic team was *preparing* to meet with my wife Julie and me in an upstairs room to deliver a series of words using the Holy Spirit gift of prophecy. We were finishing up our morning session downstairs, blissfully unaware of what the Lord was saying to this group of three people we had never laid eyes on before.

We were ushered into the upstairs room and directed to one of the many teams present in the room at that time. Our prophetic team was one of fifteen or so. Many Leaders were being ministered to that day. The team we met with didn't know our nationality, given the fact that we had registered for the event as American pastors. So, it was crazy to meet them and discover our team was Australian!

We sat down and they began to share what God had revealed to them. There were a few random words that were resonating, but they didn't ignite our spirits in the moment. And then it came.

The oldest of the three team members looked directly at me. "Mark, while praying for you I had an image come to mind. I saw you standing at the beach, and then I saw you standing on a surfboard catching waves. Mark, I feel like God is saying that in the natural you may like to surf, but in the spiritual, you are good at catching His waves and there is a wave coming that you're to catch. Moreover, I saw your car. It was a Ute done up with a bunch of surfboards, and you were carrying the surfboards for other people. You have the capacity to help other people catch the waves that you see. You are to take them with you in catching His waves. You are to lead them in that. And He is giving you the vehicle—the ministry, that allows you to empower people to catch His waves and to show them where the waves are."

Julie's head spun toward mine at the same time my head snapped toward hers. With tears flowing freely, we knew. Surfers and tsunamis. We hadn't talked about that moment since it happened, but we hadn't forgotten either.

That day God called us into the deeper waters—miracle territory. No more *mystery voice*. Now a *very familiar* voice. The voice of a heavenly Father calling us into the fullness of our identity and purpose— calling us into the deeper waters.

In a most powerful way, through the use of the Holy Spirit gift of prophecy, we were called by the voice of God to help facilitate and lead people toward what we believe is the greatest revival the world has ever seen. Since that day, we have become increasingly convinced that the global business community is a catalyst to bring this prophetic call; His Kingdom come *now*.

Anothen exists expressly for this purpose—global revival. Our surfboards are placed in the waters. We are readying and positioning ourselves like Chief Spiritual Officers (CSO's), calling and equipping Christian business leaders to think, speak, and live like heaven.

Turn your heads, the tsunami is coming! Position yourself, your family, your business today. Because if you find yourself in the right water, with the right God and the right people at the right time, you will be on the one wave that will change this generation and the course of human history forever!

"Calling all surfers. Join us in the water. There *is* a spiritual tsunami coming."

part three

Live Like Heaven

Living out the reality of thinking like heaven thinks and speaking like heaven speaks will create a new tension. That tension is nothing to fear, but is rather to be embraced. Everything of beauty is subject to perfect tension. Beautiful tension is found in a musical instrument with strings drawn taut to create a melodious sound, a canvas stretched tight across a frame so to receive the vivid colors from the artist's brush. Beautiful tension can even be found inside the barrel that is fermenting the grapes in an atmosphere of tension, in a bid to host the future wine within.

Everything of beauty is subject to perfect tension.

A beautiful life is not a life with every question satisfactorily squared away. On the contrary, it is a life that resides also in perpetual tension. Pulling down heaven to earth will bring that tension to the surface—just look at the life of Jesus!

In this final section are observations from my own journey, an attempt to wrestle honestly with the tensions of a beautiful life, a life of faith that seeks to live *like* heaven lives while in a broken world—a life of tension lived out in miracle territory.

10

A Matrix Moment

"But the time is coming—indeed it's here now—when you will be
scattered, each one going his own way, leaving me alone. Yet I am
not alone because the Father is with me. I have told you all this so
that you may have peace in me. Here on earth, you will have many
trials and sorrows. But take heart, because I have overcome the
world." (John 16:32-22)

—*Jesus of Nazareth*

The Coffee Shop

It was a Thursday, 2:13 p.m. Glancing at my calendar, I thought, "It's
hard to believe nearly 10 years have passed since my Matrix moment." I was sitting in my favorite café thinking about God, the nature
of faith, and my journey.

The coffee shop in Charlotte, North Carolina is full of people coming and going. I watch the steady stream of people, one by one, next to
the coffee stained counter. They order their drinks, stare at their phones
and wait impatiently for the energetic and cheerful barista. He clatters a
metal jug and spoon, each creation a masterpiece. Upon the announce-
ment of a name, a random person with the competitive urgency of a
Wall Street stockbroker takes his or her beverage. Each drink finds its
owner, and its way out the door, with varying degrees of temperature,
flavor, and thankfulness.

The strong aroma from years of people ordering their cup of joe permeates the atmosphere and the fibers of my clothes.

In front of the counter, separated by a half wall is the seating area. The wooden tables and chairs are the temporary grazing grounds for people who in any other arena would neither find cause nor desire to sit in such close proximity. There is the athletic girl in her early twenties writing a book report. Adjacent to her is the sneaker-wearing budding entrepreneur making a dozen calls and filling in spreadsheets. Then there's the less than ambitious businessman across from me, dressed to look more affluent than he probably is.

The two friends to the left of me are animated as they share the cares of their world, each goading the other on toward deeper expressions of concern. An older couple who earlier had taken over a corner table are now assembling a jigsaw puzzle. All the while, the silky smooth sounds of a nameless jazz musician blends with the murmuring lilts and tones of an array of indistinguishable topics.

A burst of barista steam momentarily dampens conversation. People leave, new people arrive—different faces, different anonymous lives, and the coffee shop rhythm repeats.

I looked at the older couple again and wondered if that would be Julie and me someday.

My wife Julie enjoys doing jigsaw puzzles. She will spend hours separating the edge pieces first in the quest for the corner pieces from which to reference the puzzle's frame. Once all edge pieces are in place she organizes the remaining pieces into color groups to minimize her search time later. She makes it look so easy.

When it comes to completing a jigsaw puzzle, there are two very important things you must have. The first is a clear picture to reference. The second is to make sure the pieces in the box go with the picture on the lid. In other words, make sure there is only one puzzle's worth of pieces.

If you ever want to have fun at my house, mix up the pieces of several puzzles.

Observing the comings and goings of this random selection of nameless humanity in my favorite 1000-square-foot watering hole, I was struck afresh by the life-altering discovery I made one day nearly 10 years ago.

Life is like a puzzle but most of us have messed up the pieces. On top of that, most people have either a blurred image to reference or have lost the lid altogether.

If I were to lift the lid on the life puzzle box that makes up the lives of my coffee shop companions, I am sure I'd find at least four separate puzzles. That's because I lived many years with the same four life puzzles.

The Four Life Puzzles

I have found that people tend to function through life with four different puzzles. These puzzles are a valid part of the human experience because they are the areas that are a normal part of a healthy human existence. God is in each of these puzzles because He gave us each one. There is the work puzzle, the relationship puzzle, the health puzzle, and the spiritual puzzle. And life is like having all four puzzles messed up in one box at the same time.

The work puzzle. Regardless of where we are in the corporate chain, how we feel about ourselves tends to rise and fall with the success of our work. The majority of us have had jobs in which we struggled to find satisfaction, often looking ahead for the next big opportunity, hoping that true success can be found there. Those of us who don't have jobs just want a puzzle, any puzzle, to put in the work box, if for no other reason than to feel like we fit into the bigger puzzle of our culture.

The relationship puzzle. This puzzle is as confusing as it is fulfilling. When a correct piece finally finds its home, this moment can be euphoric. Until then, sorting through the pieces of relationship turmoil can mess with one's emotional energy and stability. This puzzle is never static. It keeps changing shape and form as each year goes by. The changing nature and the potential to be wounded in the relationship puzzle can cause people to become emotionally distant, something that often occurs during relationship transitions—such as the transitions from single to married, or married to married with kids, or married with kids to an empty nest, and on it goes.

The health puzzle. The pieces of the health puzzle are many and yet all look similar. They are the pieces of ills, pills, and bills. Health puzzles are easier to talk about than they are to live. Living through health puzzle completion is monotonous. The health puzzle can thrust the existential and character questions quite unexpectedly on people. Questions such as, "Who am I and what am I here for?"

The spiritual puzzle. You know this puzzle has messed itself up and found its way into your box with all the other puzzle pieces when you begin asking, "Where is God in all of this mess?" The level of confusion created by the other three puzzles has direct impact on how we piece together God's character and nature and also how we view ourselves.

So many of us experience a minimum of four messed up puzzles. One box. One life. No lid.

Where Does Faith Fit

In relation to mergers and managers, matrimony and marriages, malady's and medicines, mystics and miracles, and any other muddled mess that makes up life—I think we have all felt the tensions that have caused us to ask ourselves the question, "Where is faith in all of this?"

We all know Hebrews 11:1,

"Now faith is confidence in what we hope for and assurance about what we do not see."(NIV).

It's a great Scripture, but the Scripture has often been given thoughtlessly to struggling people as an antidote, like a Band-Aid being offered to a victim of a life-threating injury. It's presented as a solution by those who haven't spent time with the hurting person, who haven't listened to his or her questions or truly seen that individual's pain.

There has got to be more to it than a Scripture verse.

At the risk of sounding like a politician, I will respond to the faith question with another question. "What if the separate messed up puzzles are in actual fact one puzzle and faith is a constant between all the pieces and pictures?"

Practically living out the nature of faith and the tensions surrounding it has been a worthy subject of many books, videos, conferences, and sermon series. So many have articulated over the centuries how faith is connected to trust, confidence, security, hope, miracles, and healing. Rather than attempt to write about the full depth and breadth of the subject of faith in this chapter, I want to simply share a life story. This story helped me form some conclusions about the nature of faith and yet at the same time left me with some new tensions. Here is my journey to living how heaven lives.

It's been nearly 10 years since it all began.

A Faith Story

It was a Sunday morning. My sermon was mid-preached. I could feel the rise and rhythm building to a pitch and pace that would facilitate an environment for Holy Spirit to transform lives. The body language of those listening was permissive. Their faith had been stirred.

I began to change gears, so I could land the message. I pulled away from the pulpit to emphasize my final point with a well-smithed phrase when suddenly I lost my voice. It literally felt like a clawed hand came up from deep down in my throat and took hold of my vocal chords. It felt as if they were being ripped out from the inside and dragged down to my lungs.

I choked, grabbed my throat with my left hand, and held the pulpit with my right. Tentatively I swallowed. The metal taste of blood was impossible to ignore. The congregation looked intently at me, not sure if this was part of the message or if something had gone terribly wrong. My wife could tell from my face this interruption was not in the script. I slowed my breathing down. Squeaked out a few closing remarks. Prayed. Beckoning our worship team to come up, and I sat down. Shocked. Confused. Sore. Julie, rightly asked, "What happened?" I had no idea.

I made an appointment, and two days later found myself in an ENT Specialist's chair with a scope run up my nose, so that a camera could look deep down my throat. There on the screen, the surgeon pointed to the problem, a vocal chord granuloma.

Vocal chord granulomas are fairly common. They are benign masses that grow on a vocal chord, usually because of overuse or trauma. Mine was caused by both. My vocal chords had experienced excessive use due to years of leading worship, chairing boards and committees, preaching and meetings. I had experienced a bad cold in the weeks leading up to this incident and had experienced an unusually high demand workload during the same timeframe.

My surgeon was quite excited. My case was a little unusual in that my right vocal chord had split apart and the granuloma was attempting to heal the trauma. Excitement was not an emotion I shared. The solution was to have the granuloma surgically removed.

I went back to my board that evening and very quietly explained that due to pending surgery within the next few days, I would be unable to speak well enough to lead for upwards of 10 weeks! As no doubt you are aware, 10 weeks is a long time to be absent as a leader of a complex organization. But with no other option available, and given it was a work-related injury, there was little else any of us could do but hang on for the ride.

I was about eight weeks into recovery when I began to feel like things weren't right. Each time I swallowed, I could feel something similar to a giant potato chip rubbing up and down over the affected area. I had no vocal power and was experiencing extreme pain and an increase in vocal cramping. Upon further investigation, a new granuloma was discovered. Bigger than the last!

Two more surgeries and many months of speech therapy followed with no improvement in my condition. I had gone approximately 10 months without being able to talk at all. Each time I tried, it hurt. My throat bled. My throat cramped. So, I remained silent. My puzzle pieces were all messed up!

Once again, I found myself in the chair with the dreaded scope up my nose and the now all too familiar picture on the screen. My surgeon looked at me; considerably less excited than the first time he had diagnosed me. "I have done all I know how to do. I have tried three different surgical techniques to remove the granuloma, but as you can see, it keeps reappearing. Each time with greater ferocity than the time before."

I hesitantly whispered, "What do you suggest?"

"Two options. One, you can leave it, and, realistically, you will never be able to speak properly again. Two, you can take a referral to another ENT that I know who has had a measure of success with a risky procedure using Botox. The Botox will totally paralyze the vocal chords after surgery, giving adequate time to heal. It is risky because there is a very real danger that it could remain paralyzed, meaning you may never talk in any way again."

If any well-meaning believer had tried to Hebrews 11:1 me in that moment, I would have hit them with a right cross!

Ten months of no speech for a professional verbal communicator is like being placed in solitary confinement. Seriously. The sounds of my own thoughts now ran around unharnessed in my mind. Anchors for my sanity were beginning to float adrift. Each evening's hope-filled prayers for healing were met with the following mornings searing disappointment of the first swallow of the day.

I had changed my eating habits, breathing habits, drinking habits, prayer habits, Bible reading habits, worship habits, habits, habits. Nothing was working. And while people could talk to me, actually, curiously enough they would whisper at me—like it was my hearing that was the issue, I rarely felt I could get my full meaning across. Conversation was impossible.

Ten months prior, I had been a high-quality communicator at the rising peak of my game. I had been able to articulate complex spiritual truths of the Kingdom of God in relevant ways, bringing life transformation to many. Now, I was reduced to silence. I felt useless, afraid, and internally alone. My family, friends, and church were supportive, but realistically, there was little verbal comfort they could give. After 10 months I had heard it all.

And after so many months, the world was beginning to pass me by. I was no longer invited into the day-to-day leadership decisions—my participation wasn't practical. Incidental connections with people were drying up. People were moving forward without me. More questions were rising in my spirit than I had answers for.

My puzzle pieces were everywhere and all messed in together. My lid was gone, the picture lost. My ability to care for and provide for my family, in that moment, was being taken from me. My relationship with my wife was feeling increasingly strained due to my own frustrations from not being able to speak. The existential questions became deafening as I pondered who I was becoming, "What on earth am I here for?" And the puzzle of my relationship with God was being pulled apart, muddled with the rest of my messed up life. My neat theological paradigm I had built for myself was proving utterly powerless when it really mattered most.

The rules of religious Policing were pathetic when pitted against the reality of my situation. The formulaic approaches I had previously taken to pastorally explain faith to those who suffered began to make me feel sick to the stomach. I was discovering the impotence of such formulas in my own situation. The picture I had drawn on my life's puzzle box lid had been fading and now it had disappeared completely.

That's when Jesus interrupted me. It was one of those "Matrix" moments. You know, it's when what would otherwise take years to learn becomes true for you in an instant. It's the moment in the movie where Neo learns to fight, fly a helicopter, and develop other amazing skills in seconds because of a plug connected to the back of his head.

My Matrix moment came, not unlike Neo's, while sitting in a chair—although I had a scope up my nose in place of a plug in the back of my head.

I received revelation concerning the nature of life and faith. A revelation that would help me to live from the perspective of heaven. Understanding that would normally take years, came in a moment. God revealed that I had been looking at my life as a series of separate puzzles. This had caused me to break my One God down into four gods. A god for each puzzle and each god had different faith demands.

Essentially, while life could be described as a puzzle, it was never meant to split into four.

A God For Each Puzzle

I had wrongly determined to live fractured by dividing my life into categories. Because of that, I had determined to serve four little gods.

In my *work puzzle*, god looked like a taskmaster who demanded success. I was a Policer, and good at it. My work-puzzle god reflected that. Prior to my illness, I required others to perform successfully in accordance to my religious rules. I too needed to perform successfully, in order to feel secure in my title as Chief Policer. My faith was coupled with fear. I feared retribution when tasks weren't performed to the satisfaction of my work-puzzle god's religious standards for success.

Internally I worked hard to hide my doubts about my faith lest my work-puzzle god discover that my faith wasn't big enough to meet his demands for success. In my work puzzle, I felt faith was something I had to manufacture through successful good deeds and a moral and well-disciplined life.

In my *relationship puzzle*, god was emotionally distant and I was losing emotional energy. On occasion, I could see my relationship-puzzle god's heart up close, but it only happened on those rare occasions when I had been more generous than normal, served above and beyond, or memorized a complete chapter of the Bible.

Because access to my relationship-puzzle god's emotions was conditional, my emotional connection toward others was conditional. Conditional emotional connection with others helped me preserve my emotional energy in order to stay sane.

In my Matrix moment, I saw how emotional disconnection had caused me at times to operate as a Decreaser in my attitudes toward people. I occasionally used my relationships with people as leverage to build the dream instead of using the dream to build people. It is very easy to do that when there is emotional disconnection with those we lead. A dear friend of mine, Ryan Smith, once jokingly put it this way, "God loves you and I have a perfect plan for your life!"

I found that I measured the success of my faith in my relationship puzzle by how many people liked me and did what they were told—in Jesus' name of course!

In my *health puzzle*, god looked like a teacher. I had believed health issues were given by my health-puzzle god to teach me the life lessons necessary to strengthen my character and to clarify my true identity. Health-puzzle faith led to confusion. In my understanding of my health-puzzle god's faith requirements, I wasn't being healed because I hadn't learned my life lessons yet. And it was taking a very long time for me to learn these lessons.

If I were just smart enough to learn my lessons, my problem would go away. This personal shortcoming messed with my mind, my resolve, and my identity. I felt stupid for not getting the moral of the lesson, and guilty because people could see that I wasn't getting healed, in spite of their well-meaning prayers and well wishes.

I felt exhausted because this process was taking so long. My guard was slipping. And I felt that people could see through to the real me, a person who clearly wasn't mature enough, smart enough, or had faith enough to learn his spiritual lessons.

My *spiritual-puzzle* god? He was demanding that I try to make sense of all the pieces from within my religious box. Spiritual-puzzle faith was coupled with guilt and shame. My spiritual-puzzle god saw any feelings I may have had concerning my predicament as counter-productive. Whenever I felt overwhelmed, sad, or exhausted from looking at all the pieces, or from hours looking at the blurry picture on the box, my spiritual-puzzle god would tell me to, "Straighten up and *sort* yourself out!"

Guilt and shame were residual feelings from realizing that neither my faith, mind, nor resolve were strong enough to cope with the complexity of my situation. No matter how hard I tried, I could never piece my life together to make four separate pictures!

It's Called Christian Polytheism

Christian polytheism. It sounds like a theological oxymoron, but practically speaking, Christian polytheism is how many Christians attempt to live their Christian lives today. It's certainly how I lived my life for longer than I wish to remember. Multiple puzzles, separate from each other, compartmentalized, and a different god who requires different faith for every puzzle. This way of viewing life is partly due to the Greek mindset that breaks things down into separate compartments, in order to facilitate studying and understanding them. But living from a paradigm of Christian polytheism will disable your ability to live from heaven's perspective. Christian polytheism will leave you striving toward a place you should be living from.

In my Matrix moment, it occurred to me that the more abundant life that Jesus spoke about in John 10:10 was impossible for me to experience while my view of my faith was compartmentalized. I realized that I was a Christian polytheist. My faith was compromised by fear, performance, confusion, guilt, and shame. I never allowed my multiple gods to commune with each other because that co-mingling just caused even greater confusion concerning the issues of my life and the nature of faith!

In my Matrix moment, when Jesus interrupted me, He took me back to a single picture, a clear picture, a picture that gave me permission to hold faith in tension with the struggles in my life. He revealed that I was designed to live a life that consisted not of separate puzzles but of one grand mosaic. A mosaic that is a mix of mergers and managers, Mr.'s and Mrs.'s, malady's and medicines, mystics and miracles, and any other muddled mess that makes up a life.

At the very real risk of radically oversimplifying faith, it all boiled down to one Scripture in that authentic, practical Matrix moment. Romans 3:23, *"for all have sinned and fall short of the glory of God" (NIV)*.

This Scripture gave me everything I ever needed to know about faith, God, who I am, and what I am created for—it described the picture that Jesus wanted to place on the lid of my box.

In that moment, Jesus affirmed in my human spirit that I was created to realize the fullness of being made in the image of God by living in glory with Him. Faith is what makes that possible.

In Romans 1:17 Paul put it like this,

"For in the gospel a righteousness from God is revealed, a righteousness that is by faith from first to last, just as it is written: "The righteous will live by faith"" (NIV).

The Greek words *zao ek* mean *to live and breathe out* of. Essentially, Paul says, "Faith is core to who you are." Faith is something from which we are to live.

Living from Faith

In that Matrix moment, those years ago, it became clear to me that putting the puzzle pieces of my life together as one grand mosaic was a means to an end, not an end in itself. The pieces were all there to help me build the bigger picture of becoming fully alive, *with* God, in His glory. Faith lived out in the midst of messed up pieces was a vital part of the process. Putting the grand mosaic of all the puzzle pieces together with Him would help me experience the fullness of His glory.

I have seen this idea on a parent level as well. I have sat down with my kids when they were little with puzzle pieces spread all across the table or floor. The goal of completing the puzzle was always a secondary consideration. The primary focus was quality time together. The kids definitely learned the skills of puzzle completion during those times, but, more importantly, they discovered greater understanding about my heart and love for them as their father through the process. The fullness of their life with me was enhanced by the experience of navigating the mess together.

Every generation struggles with the temptation to compartmentalize the different parts of their lives, their faith, and their God. The people of Israel were no exception. God made sure they had a firm grasp on the need to live with one picture, one faith, and one God. This exhortation can be seen in what is commonly known as the Shemar in Deuteronomy 6:4-9,

"Hear, O Israel: The Lord our God, the Lord is one. Love the Lord your God with all your heart and with all your soul and with all your strength. These commandments that I give you today are to be on your hearts. Impress them on your children. Talk about them when you sit at

*home and when you walk along the road, when you lie down and when
you get up. Tie them as symbols on your hands and bind them on your
foreheads. Write them on the doorframes of your houses and on your
gates." (NIV).*

The Hebrew word *one* is the word *echad*, meaning, *only once, once
for all.* God was making sure that His people saw no inconsistency in
Him across the different areas of their lives. He also wanted to make
sure that the generations to follow understood this unity as well. Jesus
reiterated this understanding in Matthew 22:37-38,

*" ...You must love the Lord your God with all your heart, all your
soul, and all your mind.' This is the first and greatest commandment."*

In my Matrix moment, Jesus made it clear that the amount of faith
required to be fully alive with God in His glory is not a commodity, nor
is it a product we can manufacture. Rather it is a gift *from* God and it is
sufficient. He is the source of our faith.

Romans 12:3 says,

*"Be honest in your evaluation of yourselves, measuring yourselves by
the faith God has given us."*

Looking back on the days after that Matrix moment, I see that a
new question began to form in my mind, "Can faith remain consistent
and adequately sufficient in every moment?"

Jesus makes the same curious statement pertaining to this question
several different times. One such time was when He was with the disciples in a boat in the midst of a raging storm—it was an opportunity for
the disciples to see if they possessed the faith sufficient for the moment.

*"Jesus responded, "Why are you afraid? You have so little faith!" Then
he got up and rebuked the wind and waves, and suddenly there was a*

great calm." (Matthew 8:26).

The word for *so little faith* is the Greek word, *oligopistos*, which means, *trusting too little or to have little confidence in.* In other words, Jesus refers to the *appropriation* of faith not the *quantity* of faith that the disciples possessed.

The distinction between appropriation of faith and quantity of faith is a very important one. If Jesus was referring to the quantity of faith, the disciples would have been well within their rights to say to Jesus, "Whoa, wait up a second, Jesus! You are the one who gave us the amount of faith. We can't produce it ourselves. Only You can give it. So how can you expect us to have enough faith when a major event comes our way. . . It is YOUR problem, not ours! If you want us to have more, You have to provide us with more, or, better yet, don't allow us to be in situations that require more faith than You have allocated to us."

When Jesus stated, "You have so little faith!" He was saying, "You have appropriated only a small amount of the faith I have given you, in *me*!" If that is the case, then the question has to be asked, "What were the disciples doing with the rest of their faith? Where was it hiding?"

Think of it this way. If I have a full 16-ounce cup of coffee and I pour six ounces of my coffee into an empty coffee cup, how much coffee remains in my 16-ounce cup? The answer is 10 ounces. I have only placed a *portion* of my coffee in the second cup. If I could measure faith in ounces, and using the same measurements just mentioned, with Jesus being the second cup and me being the first cup, I have only appropriated six ounces of faith in Jesus. The remaining quantity of 10 ounces is still placed in myself.

In 1 Corinthians 6:17 we read,

"But the person who is joined to the Lord is one spirit with him."

Here is the critical point of understanding: As people of righteousness, we are called to live and breathe *from faith.* We are one spirit *with*

Jesus. Faith in Jesus is to live *from* Jesus. It means to live and breathe *out* of Him. Faith is not a way of life because faith *is* life. We are designed to live *from* heaven.

Faith *is* life in Christ. It is seen when Paul is speaking to the Galatian church in Galatians 2:20,

"My old self has been crucified with Christ. It is no longer I who live, but Christ lives in me. So I live in this earthly body by trusting in the Son of God, who loved me and gave himself for me."

The word, *trusting* comes from the Greek word, *pistis*. It means, *holy fervor, born of faith and joined with it*. I can never *live in* the fullness of the more abundant life if I don't *live from* the fullness of the more abundant life. I can never live *by* faith in Jesus Christ if I don't live *from* faith in Jesus Christ.

If faith comes from one consistent good source, then it can be assumed there is consistency and adequacy of the faith given. There is no area or moment in your life that you don't have an immediate and adequate resource of faith. You can live from faith in Jesus all the time—faith is a state of being.

Two Questions

For so long, I used faith sporadically as a reaction to an event. I didn't live from it. Like throwing water on a fire, I chose to have faith intersect with a given moment rather than to *live by faith*. But in that Matrix moment, Jesus began to reveal to me that faith was not a reaction to a moment, but rather a constant in every moment.

I began to realize that the events of my life needed to intersect with my faith and not the other way around. Also, I discovered that I didn't have to use my faith one way for one circumstance and another way for another circumstance. One picture. One faith. One God.

While unable to speak, I sat in that chair, while God downloaded revelation concerning my faith and all my puzzle pieces, I heard two questions come to my spirit:

"Mark, where are you appropriating your faith?"

and

"Are you living from Jesus?"

We say it all the time, "You need to have faith in your own abilities," or, "That person must have a lot of faith in themselves to have done such and such."

So often, like the disciples, I was living from myself, only appropriating a small amount of my God-given faith in Jesus and then hoping that I had enough faith in Jesus when my faith was confronted by the intersections of my life. I was placing my faith in my abilities. I was not living from faith in Jesus. I was living from faith in me.

I repented.

I decided there and then that, no matter what came next, I would appropriate all of my faith in Jesus and live from Him. I decided to trust Jesus with my whole life. The mosaic was about one faith and one God, and I decided to put the practice of Christian polytheism behind me once for all. It was time for me to be fully alive with God, in His glory, regardless of the many and varied circumstances that made up my life.

Two more operations would follow. A further eight months of not knowing where things would end up, a total of one-and-a-half years with no voice before I was healed. But I did receive a miracle.

The miracle was not so much that my vocal issues were resolved immediately; the miracle was that eight months prior to being restored to health, I was able to trust God completely with every aspect of my life. I was living *from* a new place.

The miracle of that Matrix moment enabled my faith to be an adequate constant, spanning the full spectrum of my life. My faith was no longer activated by fear, performance, confusion, guilt, or shame. My faith became a constant of trust, confidence, security, and hope.

My faith became the constant that intersected with life events. Embracing the revelation of that Matrix moment meant that miracle territory would no longer be reduced to one or two *compartments* of my life. Walking in miracle territory was now my *whole* life.

Living from Jesus, living from a life of faith has created a new paradox of feeling scared and liberated all at the same time. It is like sweet and sour chicken or salted caramel, tensions of taste that awaken sensations through surprise. Living from Jesus became the catalyst for me moving from Policer to Releaser. Policers implode in perpetual tension, but, in the tension between scared and liberated, Releasers become fully alive!

A further eight months with no voice and unanswered questions couldn't control the appropriation of my faith. The miracle was that, in spite of a significant tension between fear and liberation existing in my life, by faith I was living *from* God *with* God *in* His glory—fully alive, living how heaven lives!

Five Questions to Consider Concerning the Nature of Your Faith

Here are five questions for you to consider concerning the nature of your faith in your personal, family, and business life:

1. Does your Christian life feel different in your work, family, health, and your spiritual life?

2. Is faith easier to apply in some parts of your life than others?

3. Do you relate to God differently in the different areas of your life?

4. When life gets out of control, does this chaos or uncertainty affect your view of God's character and nature?

5. Does living like Jesus seem to be more about some new set of

behaviors than a heart encounter?

If you answered yes to the majority of these questions, then you may well be living a life of Christian polytheism, a life made up of different compartments, each with its own puzzle to complete.

We have all been invited to live in life's tension *from* faith, to live in the fullness that comes from thinking and speaking like heaven. I know from personal experience that faith can be a constant in the midst of tension.

Now Faith Is Being Sure

Just for the record, I love the definition of faith found in Hebrews 11:1,

"Now faith is being sure of what we hope for and certain of what we do not see."

The word *being sure* is the Greek word, *hypostasis*, meaning, *foundation, a substance, a real being*. It is the right definition because it reminds us that the true potential of faith is only fully activated when placed in and lived entirely from the person who gave it—Jesus. He is the only one who sees the full mosaic of our lives. He knows what is being built and how all the areas work together day by day, moment by moment, event by event to establish His Kingdom in our lives.

I still have faith questions. I still wonder why good people who appropriate their faith well have to die before what seems to be their time. I wonder why some people who appropriate their faith well get healed and others don't. I have questions regarding why some of my well-appropriated faith-filled prayers get answered and others appear unheard. There are still tensions in my understanding and experience of faith. And the longer I live from faith appropriated in Jesus, I am increasingly okay with the tensions.

It's hard to believe nearly 10 years have passed since I was healed in my thinking and since the surgery that allowed me to speak again. Ten years of living in a new faith reality. Ten years of living without faith being a formula. Ten years of using the many experiences of my life to build one picture, with one faith, and one God. Ten years of learning how to live *from* a faith in Jesus that produces trust, confidence, security, and hope.

Don't get me wrong, there have plenty of other trials, new tensions. And as each trial intersects with my faith I can still feel my old self-made puzzle gods attempt to resurrect themselves, looking for another opportunity to control my faith appropriation. But I only have to stop momentarily and remember the way they caused me to react from fear, performance, confusion, guilt, and shame before I shut them down.

Faith is a lived-out story—your story, my story. It is a lived-out story that is made up of work puzzles, relationship puzzles, health puzzles, and spiritual puzzles. The puzzles overlap, they intertwine, they share pieces, but they are all one.

No matter who you are, your lived-out story, like the stories of the people sitting in my favorite 1000-square-foot coffee shop, is a story of triumph, trials, and the tension of faith. Don't spend the rest of your days attempting to live in separate compartments; stop putting all your faith in yourself. Trust me. Doing so will do your head in!

Instead, I invite you to live life as a Releaser in miracle territory, *from* faith in Jesus, allowing Him to piece your life together. Take some time right now and put your total faith in Him in order to live from Him. No compartments. One picture. He is calling you to be released into the fullness of His glory by inviting you to live from heaven's perspective.

II

Love Lived Out- KRI's

"Once you are real you can't become unreal again. It lasts for always."

—*Velveteen Rabbit*

The Setup

It was 1996. The year Prince Charles and Princess Dianna were divorced, Kofi Annan was elected to be the United Nations' seventh secretary-general, and anything from Eric Clapton, Jamiroquai, and Snoop Dog could be heard on the radio. It was also the year the Dow ended over the 6000 mark, 35 people were killed in the Port Arthur massacre in Tasmania, the Cowboys beat the Steelers 27-17 at Sun Devil Stadium to win Super bowl XXX, and the XXVI Summer Olympic Games took place in Atlanta, Georgia.

That is where I found myself. July, at ground zero of world sport. But I wasn't there for the Olympics. As big as the Olympics were, in my world at that time, a bigger game was about to be played. It was a game between two mighty powers. The triune God and my will!

While I loved being around people, prior to 1996, I had never been a person who cared too much for deep relationships. In essence, the

"Me" people saw and the "Me" I was when away from people were very different. My wife of three years and I were exploring new levels of relational intimacy with each other, but I had few friends and even fewer acquaintances. I was, however, a pragmatist. Reasoning showed me that leveraging relationships was important in order to complete a task, and so I did my best to be friendly and affable in most situations without ever giving too much of my inner self away.

Traveling to Atlanta from Australia was one of the leveraging opportunities I had been looking for. I was seeking to build a broader network of connections as I was sensing a leaning toward itinerate ministry sometime in the future. My friend, Joey, was taking a preaching trip and asked if I would travel with him to play piano and sing at each of his speaking engagements.

Joey had seen something in me that I hadn't. He had seen my *real* relational potential, the authentic me that I tried to hide. While he did need me to serve alongside him for the three weeks we would be there, I think he had a greater agenda that I was unaware of at the time.

He suggested that I head out to Atlanta a week before him, and that I should stay with a good pastor friend of his. The rationale he gave me was that I would learn some good leadership skills from his friend, I would meet some interesting people, and it would be good for me to put myself in a foreign environment without anyone familiar around. I agreed.

What I didn't realize is that Joey had placed me for an entire week in close community with a man of God who oozed shepherding gifts! Joey's pastor friend was highly relational and was someone who was adept at connecting with people in ways that went well beyond a surface relationship. He was *real*. He was the kind of authentic person that freaked me out! I would typically avoid *real* people, lest I found myself revealing more of my inner thoughts and feelings than I felt comfortable with.

This was a good old-fashioned setup.

I will never forget the first night I arrived. I flew into Hartsfield-Jackson Atlanta Airport and was greeted warmly by Joey. Outside of trying to get into the wrong side of the car, the trip too was pretty standard. It was filled with the cursory stories about long flights and the basic observable differences between Australia and what I was seeing in this new country. I was looking forward to stopping and settling down in my own room for a while.

That didn't happen.

When we arrived at the house there was a phone message waiting. A member of the pastor's congregation, who was in hospice care, had taken a turn for the worse. The family was requesting the pastor's presence for what would be the dying man's final hours.

Quite honestly, one of the reasons I liked the idea of itinerant ministry at the time was, in my immature estimation, the seeming lack of opportunity for being near people in deep need, especially sick people. Need can be messy, and the idea that I could fly into a new city, speak, and then move on was appealing.

This was an itinerant ministry trip, and I respectfully declined the invitation to join the pastor's hospice visit.

And that is when Joey's true agenda for my being in Atlanta a week early was revealed.

The clash of powers. The power of God in one corner represented through my *real* host, and the power of my will in the other. We went toe-to-toe in his living room for several drawn out minutes as he declared in no uncertain terms that I *would* be attending this visit with him.

He spoke calmly but sternly. He had been charged with the responsibility of providing spiritual growth opportunities for me while I was there, and this was one of them. Equally stern but with less calm, I threw back at him my lack of desire to go anywhere near sick people. I was young. I was scared. This was too *real* for me.

However, after several rounds of verbal sparring, I yielded. After all, he was the owner of the bed I hoped to sleep in and the provider of the food I hoped to eat. Reluctantly, I returned to the car, correct side this time, and headed out with him into the rainy night.

As I opened the squeaky door, I was introduced to what I had feared. The hospice facility was everything I had expected. The lights were yellow and dim. The walls, pale and green, and the air carried a mildly musty scent, the kind that hangs in your nostrils long enough to taste. We walked a long corridor. At its end in the last room on the left, subtle sobs could be heard—that was our room.

Everything within me wanted to turn and run. With every sob my steps grew shorter. This was getting way too real way too quick for my liking. Yet what was about to unfold in that small square room would forever change my view of people and the purpose of relationships in the Kingdom of God.

In the bed was a very frail and unwell man. Sitting in the five chairs surrounding the bed were the man's immediate family. As I stood at the entrance to the room, I could feel hopelessness in the air. No platitude or glib remark would ease their tension or pain. There was no plan or sequence of events that would change the outcome. This man was about to leave this life. Pragmatism was of no use here. Only the authenticity of relationship at the deepest level could bring any hope in this most unpleasant space. It would take someone who was relationally *real* to change this atmosphere.

And that is what happened. In the ensuing hours, I learned from a Releaser—a relationship master, the power of the Kingdom metric. This Kingdom metric helped me to see in tangible ways what it meant to live from the perspective of heaven. It would be quite some years later before I would fully realize the true impact of what I saw that night. What took place is what I now refer to as *KRIs: Key Relationship Indicators*.

Key Relational Indicators

KRIs fall under the umbrella of love. After all, as we have already seen, Paul makes it clear that we are to make love our highest goal. The Key Relational Indicators are,

- Honor (Who I Am)
- Respect (Who You Are)
- Dignity (Protecting Who You Are)
- Creativity (Calling Out Who You Are)

In the immediate context of my Atlanta hospice experience, the KRIs were employed in the following way:

Honor. As soon as the pastor entered the room, he began to thank God that He was present, that He was good, and that He had invited us all into a most holy moment. It was also verbalized that we were invited because we were His children and He was our Father. He emphasized that we were honored to be invited by God to take part in this valuable day in the dying man's life.

Honor bought the reality of heaven's perspective to the people present. Immediately the atmosphere in the room changed. Hopelessness shifted to a growing sense of security. Someone was in the room who was secure in their identity, knew what they were doing, wanted to be there, and could be trusted to steward the moment well. Honor is being real about our true identity as sons and daughters of the Father. It recognizes that even though we each have a role to play, no one of us is any more powerful than anyone else. Honor recognizes the value of who we are.

Respect. Respect was shown by asking heart questions of the people present, questions that demonstrated that the pastor was not afraid of people's emotions, and that emotions had a place to be heard. Respect gives permission for people to be emotionally real. Respect looks at the whole person.

After listening actively to the hearts of the people and what they were feeling, the pastor then asked questions that spoke to some of their real physical needs, such as rest, food, and coffee. Respect says, "I see all of the real you right now, and what you are feeling has value."

Dignity. Dignity was revealed when the dying man was kissed on the brow by the pastor and by the care he took as he held the dying man's hand, and stroked his hair. Even though something was obviously wrong, it didn't change the way the pastor treated the man.

Dignity was also on display by the way the pastor spoke. He didn't speak as though the dying man wasn't there. Dignity brings value to people by protecting who they are. Dignity said in that moment, "Even at the point of your most vulnerable, you are an image-bearer of God and that matters to me. I will do all within my power to protect that."

Dignity is treating a person as a real and whole person, just how Jesus would treat a person, no matter what has transpired. Dignity is ready to realign any faulty understanding of identity.

Creativity. Creativity was released as members of the family were given opportunity and permission to remember the narrative of the man's life. The pastor and those in the room remembered life events and were calling out the weak man's identity.

Creativity speaks life by declaring how an individual has helped to *create* a very real and positive experience in the lives of those in relationship with them. Creativity didn't deny the situation at hand. It released life into the atmosphere by subtly reminding people that their loved one was not defined by his current state, but rather defined by who he was as made in the image of God and the real consequential effect that his life had on others.

KRIs Before KPIs

Key Performance Indicators (KPIs) have been a well-known metric to help businesses and organizations assess the success or failure of human performance as it pertains to the attainment of reaching pre-defined organizational goals. KPIs are important and help considerably to enhance organizational efficiency, effectiveness, and to produce healthy ROIs (Returns On Investment). However, as necessary as they are, KPIs by their very nature are a performance metric and are fundamentally different than Key Relational Indicators (KRIs).

While KPIs are about performance, KRIs are about love. KRI's reveal love in action and inspire in people the desire to be real, to live authentically, and to be fully released into living from the fullness of the Kingdom of God. KRIs are the practical metrics of heaven that help us know that we are definitely living how heaven lives. Performance is only transformational if love is the foundation from which you perform.

The fact is, the pastor who visited hospice that night had a job to perform outside of ministering to the dying man. In that larger role as pastor of a congregation, he wanted a positive, measurable outcome. He wanted to see church growth from his efforts. Those were his KPIs, but he wasn't operating from a desire to see those metrics met, he was operating from something much more powerful, much more authentic. He was operating from a greater metric. His Releaser's heart was all about relationship.

You see, even though KPIs can include a relational metric, they are ultimately more mechanistic than relational. They speak of bottom lines, deltas, and net worth outcomes. KPIs are valuable and necessary, but they fall short of Kingdom outcomes if used outside of authentic relationships.

The pastor's ultimate goal that night was to host the presence of God. He was there to strengthen the relationship between six people and their God—pull heaven down to earth. In other words, he was there for love. And because of this motivation, he was able to establish and then maintain an atmosphere where everyone had access to trust. He was able to reveal truth in a way that hurting hearts could hear.

KRIs do what KPI's can never do. They invite people into a safe place where they can be real with themselves, with their God, and with each other. And what's amazing is when a love relationship is the goal, the bi-product, as revealed to me by the pastor's time with this particular family, was the successful attainment of his KPI targets.

Our Position Before Our Purpose

KPIs are based on *performance* in relation to the set rules established by an organization in order to control culture and deliver a preferred outcome. KRIs are based on our *position* as a son or daughter of the Father. KRIs in action inspire in people the desire to be authentic, to be real.

The metric of the world is performance based. The metric of the Kingdom is relationally based. The performance metric of the world is diametrically opposed to the relational metric of the Kingdom.

The metric used in any given context is determined by the governmental structure placed in authority over that context. The governance of the context of earth is control through elected representatives who legislate order with rules. The governance of heaven is family—a Father who sends His Son to find a Bride who is wooed by the Holy Spirit.

Performance keeps people in a pseudo-reality by control. Kingdom relationships release people into their *real* identity with love. For Kingdom business to fulfill its mandate, the measurement for success must be based primarily on our relational position as a son or daughter, not the legislative measure of compliance with the rules.

John put it this way in John 15:5,

"Those who remain in me, and I in them will produce much fruit. For apart from me you can do nothing."

The Greek word for *remain* is *meno*. It carries three elements concerning relationship.

- Proximity. Not to depart from a given place but rather to remain present with another.
- Time. Not to give up but to endure together.
- Condition. Remain in a state of connection and unity with another.

In these two brief sentences, Jesus eloquently ties the connection between relationship and task, KRI and KPI.

Paul builds on this theme in Ephesians 2:10,

"For we are God's masterpiece. He has created us anew in Christ Jesus, so we can do the good things he planned for us long ago."

The Greek word for created is, *ktizo*. It means, *complete change and transformation*. This change is not just spiritual, but, as seen in previous chapters, it is a positional one and therefore a relational one.

Paul connects the dots between our position and our purpose in the following ways:

- God did "this," so we could do "that."
- We could not do "that" before He did "this."
- God doing "this" for us has now given us the necessary potential to do "that."

Our potential is based on our position not our performance, and our potential is secured by love and cannot be altered by any force, neither human nor spiritual.

"Neither death nor life, neither angels nor demons, neither our fears for today nor our worries about tomorrow—not even the powers of hell can separate us from God's love" (Romans 8:38).

Isn't that awesome?

We have a new position in God initiated by, and then secured by, His always perfect love.

We are being released to be real, to live relationally authentic in every area of life. Our purpose is discovered in our position as a son or daughter of heaven. We may fulfill a task but without a love relationship, this task is nothing more than what Paul refers to in 1 Corinthians 13:1 as a "clashing cymbal;" it's just noise, and success will inevitably be determined by a new set of rules to measure it.

The task is always a means to an end. The end is always to be released into a greater love connection with God and subsequently a greater love connection with each other. The end is that we would live real existences, authentic in love before God and each other. The greater we live authentically in our Kingdom relationships, the greater we maximize our Kingdom fruit-bearing potential.

John captures this notion when he recalls Jesus' pronouncement of His impending death in John 13:34-35,

> *"So now I am giving you a new commandment: Love each other. Just as I have loved you, you should love each other. Your love for one another will prove to the world that you are my disciples."*

Notice that there is no mention of building big buildings, performing lots of well-meaning tasks, or even having a well-defined vision or theology. There's no mention of gifted teachers articulating to the masses. All of those things are great, but the metric for Kingdom success is non-linear. It *is* relational. It *is* about love—it is discovered when we are released to live powerfully authentic lives when we get real.

A Tale of Two Currencies

There are two distinctly different sets of currencies: the currency of earth and the currency of heaven. For a business to bear fruit that produces Kingdom currency, it needs a new set of assumptions. A whole new rubric needs to be implemented—a business needs to operate under the banner of love with heaven's Key Relationship Indicators.

KRIs transform earthly currency into Kingdom currency, the storing up of true riches in heaven, as seen in Matthew 6:19-21,

"Don't store up treasures here on earth, where moths eat them and rust destroys them, and where thieves break in and steal. Store your treasures in heaven, where moths and rust cannot destroy, and thieves do not break in and steal. Wherever your treasure is, there the desires of your heart will also be."

When KRIs are the foundational approach to business, KPIs can become powerful tools. But if you try and do it the other way around, you will never experience the full measure of your mandate—*"on earth as it is in heaven."*

Years ago, I took a counseling class that required I visit a crematorium. My classmates and I were learning about the systems and processes of burial, so to better help grieving families. I find crematoriums to be rather macabre environments. No matter how nicely the red curtains hang, how soft the music plays, or how lovely the flower arrangements, everybody knows what goes on there. But as unsettling as they may be, crematoriums are also fascinating places.

Our guide took us *out back* to where all the furnaces were. One of our classmates noticed a large green plastic trash bin at the end of one of the furnaces and asked why it was there. The guide shared how the titanium used in surgical implants doesn't melt and therefore needs to be discarded using other means. At the end of a cremation cycle, the metal parts are *collected* and placed in the green bin until there are enough of them to send outside to a hole in the ground where they would be buried and forgotten.

We all peeked tentatively over the top of the bin.

While there were enough parts of various shapes and sizes to make a rather convincing robot, it was something else that caught my eye. There, at the bottom of the pile, was a charred coin. Even though I had always known, "You can't take it with you when you go," the truth of that adage penetrated my heart when I saw that lonely coin.

Standing in that place where the end of life is just another day at the office, there was no escaping the reality that the very best attempts to transition physical resources from earth to heaven fall hopelessly short.

Kingdom currency and earthly currency are two *different* things. Even if we wanted to store up for ourselves earthly treasures in heaven, we simply cannot. So, what are the treasures that we can store? They are the treasure of eternal love relationships.

In the love relationship between God and people and between sons and daughters, love is the currency of the Kingdom. By using earthly resources to facilitate the love connection between God and people, and God's people to one another, we convert earthly currency to Kingdom currency.

The relationship between earthly currency and Kingdom currency acts similarly to the physics behind the electrical transformer principle.

An electrical transformer transforms electricity from one amount of voltage to another. The input voltage and the output voltage remain electrically isolated from each other. Inside the transformer are two separate coils of wire that **are not physically connected to each other in any way.** They are, however, connected magnetically via a soft-iron core that runs around and through both coils. As electricity passes through coil number one, a magnetic field is generated that transfers through the iron core to coil number two, either increasing or decreasing the amount of voltage as the magnetism converts back to electricity through coil number two. For example, let's say there are 10 volts of electricity going through 100 turns of wire in coil number one, and there are 1000 turns of wire in coil number two. The magnetism generated from the voltage in coil number one is picked up by the iron core, which then transfers that energy to coil number two (Remember—the wire coils are not joined physically). Because there are more turns of wire in coil number two, as this wire picks up the magnetism from the iron core it increases the electricity value times ten. In other words, we started with 10 volts in coil number one and will end up with 100 volts coming through coil number two. Storing up treasures in heaven is a similar principle. In like fashion, we are physically isolated from heaven, but *spiritually* connected. There is nothing *physically* connecting us to heaven. However, we are spiritually connected because the Holy Spirit lives *in* us, spiritually connecting the physical us on earth to the spiritual heaven. Therefore, what we build here on earth, in terms of Kingdom love relationships, has a direct transferable impact on the spiritual treasure we store in heaven.

When Kingdom business allows KPIs to connect to the presence of God through KRIs, earthly currency is transferred and converted to Kingdom currency. It can be measured in the quantity of people who are restored to healthy love relationship with God. That is His original intent—to restore people to His glory in order for them to be fully alive, real, authentic in love.

The Divine Relationship

The Genesis account of creation, as found in Genesis 1 and 2, and Colossians 1, provides a wonderful archetype of how KRIs should be used in leadership, management, and business. No one has ever done the job quite like God. Everything God did was good, and it was all about a love relationship with us.

From the beginning, God had a strategy to bring order to chaos—

to create.

The words, *formless and void*, in Genesis 1, are the Hebrew words, *tohu* and *bohu*, which mean topsy-turvy. God remained in a healthy relationship with Himself during the process of bringing order and then invited others into His orderly relationship. And there was never a point in the entire creation process where God was not love.

The results were measurable. "God said . . . And there was." And He worked from rest and revealed that rest is key to maintaining healthy relationships. We all need a regular Sabbath.

Throughout the whole creative process, the KRIs of honor, respect, dignity, and creativity were present.

Honor: All three members of the Trinity operated perfectly from the fullness of their identity--love. The Apostle John emphasized this in his first letter,

"But anyone who does not love does not know God, for God is love" *(1 John 4:8).*

It took teamwork. The Father spoke. Colossians 1:15-20 shows Jesus as the physical Creator. And Holy Spirit hovered over the earth. There was no threat by any member to another. No one member was seen as more powerful than the others. They operated in differing roles toward the common and good purpose of creating opportunity for bearers of His image to come into relationship with Himself.

Respect: The nature of the Divine love relationship can be seen under pressure in the Garden of Gethsemane in Luke 22:42-44,

"'Father, if you are willing, please take this cup of suffering away from me. Yet I want your will to be done, not mine.' Then an angel from heaven appeared and strengthened him. He prayed more fervently, and he was in such agony of spirit that his sweat fell to the ground like great drops of blood."

Jesus had permission to express His emotions and the Father sent an angel who attended to His physical and emotional needs. Jesus was being real in the garden. The mandate was fulfilled but not at the expense of the emotions that expressed Jesus' humanity in the process.

The initial creative act and the ongoing work of creation reveal that God sees everything and everyone. Colossians 1:17 reveals Christ is still holding all things together; therefore, nothing sits outside of His attention. God sees the whole person.

Dignity: In Genesis 1:26-31, on the final day of creation, God creates humanity. It was a collective creative work that resulted in a created being that reflected the three members of the Trinity,

"Then God said, "Let us make human beings in our image, to be like us."

In contrast to the creation of the heavens, earth, oceans, foliage, and animals, God declares the creative work, *"very good"* or *meh·ōde* in the Hebrew. This word is a declaration that goodness has now been revealed in abundance.

Dignity comes from image and choice. Control chips away choice and, therefore, is an affront to the image of God. Control is the antithesis of a healthy love relationship because controlled people aren't released to act from a place of authenticity. God gave us dignity by creating us with the power to choose, just as He chooses. Free will is a moot point if choice is absent.

Genesis 9:5-6 reinforces the value of the image of God. Under the Old Covenant, there were great consequences for anyone who took a human life--an attack on His image-bearers equates to an attack on Himself. Nothing is of greater value than God, and therefore, the replication of His image in us carries dignity of the highest order.

Creativity: Value and meaning come from story. The fact that God chronicled the act of creation, the history of His dealings with His people throughout the ages, and prophecy concerning end times, affirms this conclusion. Through His-story, God has revealed there is a grand narrative playing out. Meaning comes from our involvement in that narrative. Such meaning is apparent when God invited Adam into the creation narrative in Genesis 2:19,

"So the Lord God formed from the ground all the wild animals and all the birds of the sky. He brought them to the man to see what he would call them, and the man chose a name for each one."

Creativity is revealed in God's invitation to humanity to participate with God in the story. And just prior, in verse 18, we see that the invitation involved relationship,

"Then the Lord God said, "It is not good for the man to be alone. I will make a helper who is just right for him."

God declared that when man is not in an authentic image-bearing relationship, the situation is something less than good. To not be in such a relationship is to not participate fully in the image of God.

The Kingdom love relationship triangle illustrates this concept perfectly. The top joining point of the triangle is God. The bottom left and right joining points are people in relationship with each other. The closer they grow in intimacy with God, the closer they grow in relationship with each other. The greater the intimacy, the greater the authenticity, the greater the love connection.

Being made in God's image is to be made for a love relationship. God is in a love relationship with Himself as Father, Son, and Holy Spirit, because He is love. A Kingdom love relationship is the creative force generated when one person's story intersects with another's and those two stories create something new.

God never struggled for creativity and didn't get writer's block at the end of day six! After the creative process of working as a team to produce the heavens, earth, and sustainable life, He then released a plan to draw all humanity back into an authentic love relationship with

Himself.

KRIs and the Decreasers, Policers, and Releasers

Over the past twenty years, I have observed that the Kingdom use of KRIs is never welcome in a culture of control. Controlling environments create a pseudo-reality concerning trust, truth, and intimacy. At very best, Decreaser and Policer environments will focus on one or more KRI elements for a season to establish or regain control.

I once saw an insightful infographic delineating some of the differences between a boss and a leader. It illustrated well what I believe to be the general differences between Decreasers and Policers who tend to be bosses, and Releasers who tend to be leaders:

A boss:
- Is impersonal
- Says "I"
- Uses people
- Inspires fear
- Takes credit
- Micromanages
- Says, "You Go"
- Thinks short-term
- Is your "Boss"
- Focuses on process

A leader:
- Is compassionate
- Says, "We"
- Develops people
- Earns respect
- Gives credit

- Delegates
- Says, "Let's Go"
- Thinks long-term
- Is your colleague
- Focuses on people

Decreaser bosses tend to use various KRI elements as tools of manipulation to achieve a selfish purpose. Decreasers develop non-submissive environments. Such environments build a culture of suspicion that can become a breeding ground for emotional burnout.

Bill Johnson, from Bethel Church, recently said, "Flattery is counterfeit honor." Decreasers cultivate distorted cultures of honor that point toward themselves because counterfeit honor toward Decreasers is the air used to puff up their own pride. Decreasers will also use KRI terms such as, "respectfully," like a Trojan horse to unleash a manipulative agenda through shame, guilt, and fear.

Dignity for the Decreaser is a tool used to drip-feed hope within an organization. It is used sparingly after relational turmoil to shore up a cracking leadership façade. It gives false hope that the Decreaser truly cares about the members of the team.

Creativity is a form of false humility for the Decreaser. Decreasers will say nice things about people all the while thinking quite the opposite. They will use creativity to establish a false connection while shifting attentions away from their plotting and scheming.

Policer bosses submit to God's authority while not accessing His power, and typically reduce the mandate of the Kingdom to those things that can be done in the natural. Therefore, Policer boss environments tend to use KRI elements to ensure predictable outcomes that stabilize organizational control because success for the Policer is partly measured by how well people in the organization follow the rules.

Honor is positional, and everyone can be honored in a Policing boss environment but only to the point of ensuring those within the organization honor the leader above everyone else. This practice ensures the Policer's control. The same is true of respect. Policers will show respect to a person until that person shows his or her potential to be more powerful than the Policer. Then respect turns on a dime toward mistrust.

Dignity has a timeframe for a Policer. The Policer is happy to protect who you are while you are not actively sinning. But sin undermines a Policer's rules. Therefore, the Policer boss's leadership style is the carrot and the stick. By offering relationship acceptance to people who follow the rules, Policers bring rule breakers back into relationship with the rules. The absence of dignity is evident in this environment.

Creativity is very present in Policer boss environments, but it has parameters. Policers will not call out what is inside a person beyond the scope of what the Policer's own leadership capacity can handle. In some British Colonies, this practice is known as the *Tall Poppy Syndrome*. When a person within the pack rises too high above the rest, he or she is cut back down to the level of the whole.

Healthy Kingdom love relationships cannot be legislated; they begin with transformation of who you are. *You* must be *real* before your relationships become authentic. That is why the art of learning who you are and operating from your true identity as a son or daughter of heaven is of key importance.

People are not machines. People are the image-bearers of God. How you think determines how you feel, which determines how you act. Treat people like machines and they will speak like machines and act like machines.

But if you desire a Kingdom business that fulfills heaven's mandate and releases the power of the Kingdom of God upon the earth, then you need to think how heaven thinks, speak how heaven speaks and live how heaven lives. Be real and authentic--a Releaser who uses the Kingdom metric of KRIs to create a real Kingdom culture of love.

God Has Won

In 1996 the phone rang in Queensland. It was a late afternoon in mid-July.

"God has won," I said in response to my wife Julie's question concerning what I had been up to since arriving in Atlanta.

"What do you mean?" She asked.

"Last night I got to be a part of something that gave me greater job satisfaction than anything I have ever been part of."

Then, with tears streaming down my face, I told her the story of a pastor who revealed the power of God's love through authentic relationship. And how I witnessed a frail man pass from this life to the next with honor, respect, dignity, and love.

That experience revealed God's love working through the Kingdom principle of KRIs. It changed the trajectory of my future. Honor, dignity, respect, and creativity are the Key Relationship Indicator's under the umbrella of love. They are not management principles. They are the hallmarks of authenticity; they are *life* and *real* life more abundantly.

KRIs in action was the vehicle of love God used to wake me up and bring me to life. KRIs in action unlocked in me the desire to explore and question the tensions of life and love in new ways.

God is battling for your leadership heart. As a catalytic leader and image-bearer of God, you have the power to choose who you will be. A Decreaser? A Policer? Or a Releaser? And you have the power to determine whether your environment will measure success from the perspective of earth or the perspective of heaven. The power of choice is in your hands. Which do you choose?

Putting It All Together

I have always loved the story of the *Velveteen Rabbit*. It's the story of the journey from pretend to real. In a spiritual sense, the Velveteen Rabbit is a great allegory of the journey from old to new, dead to fully alive in God. A child's toy in the story explains this phenomenon:

"Real isn't how you are made," said the Skin Horse. "It's a thing that happens to you. When a child loves you for a long, long time, not just to play with, but REALLY loves you, then you become Real."

"Does it hurt?" asked the Rabbit.

"Sometimes," said the Skin Horse, for he was always truthful. "When you are Real you don't mind being hurt."

"Does it happen all at once, like being wound up," he asked, "or bit by bit?"

"It doesn't happen all at once," said the Skin Horse. "You become. It takes a long time. That's why it doesn't happen often to people who break easily, or have sharp edges, or who have to be carefully kept. Generally, by the time you are Real, most of your hair has been loved off, and your eyes drop out and you get loose in the joints and very shabby. But these things don't matter at all, because once you are Real you can't be ugly, except to people who don't understand."

The process to *real* has been a long and winding one for me. Quite literally, the process to real as taken me to the ends of the earth. And it has happened in the most unlikely of places and been initiated by the most unlikely of people.

Put simply, the process to real is arriving at a place of thinking, speaking, and living *from* heaven's perspective.

Thinking How Heaven Thinks

We cannot hope to know what to speak or how to live until we understand the sounds of truth to which we need to align our thinking.

Unbeknownst to him, Gary helped me to understand that God does speak to me through His Word. It was my encounter in a Toy World store all those many years ago, that Holy Spirit used to shore up my identity later in life by refining what it meant for me to live out of a new position as a royal priest and explore the implications of my new potential as a mobile temple. Reflecting on my time working with Australia's biggest private company, I discovered that my new position and potential gave me access to new power, but in order to access that power, I first had to choose if I would be a Decreaser, Policer, or a Releaser. We had never planned for our 10th Wedding Anniversary to become a defining moment that would develop into a teaching tool regarding the "What" of the Kingdom of God. And I could be quite certain that neither Pastor Laurie, Jason Clark, nor John Rowley were going about their days hoping I would learn the relationship between love, truth, trust and the Trinity—but that's what occurred.

Thinking about who I am from the perspective of heaven has been a total shift in how I hear truth. I shifted from viewing myself through the lens of religious rules to now viewing myself the way our Father sees me—a royal son who is eternally connected to a heavenly family, who gets to live in two places at once and bring heaven to earth.

Speaking How Heaven Speaks

Being a husband and parent has taken me to depths in relationship I never knew were possible. And as I have plumbed these depths over the past 23 years I have realized the absurdity of my previous belief system that God doesn't speak to us apart from His Word. Through my years in relationship with family, it is much clearer to me now that I am made in the image of God to be relational as He is relational. What is also clearer is His heart to want to relate *to* me and *through* me to others using all of His creation as a tool to do that.

Speaking how heaven speaks has required a whole new level of purpose toward spending time in the Word of God. As communicators of the conversations of heaven, it is incumbent upon us to be sure we have our thinking aligned right with what heaven is saying through the Word of God before we open our mouths!

My Mum revealed that her thinking was right that night in a pizza store in North Carolina, where a little boy named Jimmy and his mum were reminded that God does see them and loves them because of her decision to release a word of knowledge in love. Bill had his thinking right when he encouraged me to ask questions about God's nature and character in order to help me live from a place of spiritual strength by receiving the good gift of tongues from my always perfect Father. And an Aussie prophet in Northern California had his thinking right the day he saw in the spirit, a surfer preparing to catch a wave of revival, the likes of which has never been seen before—and then spoke that over my life.

Speaking how heaven speaks has changed the purpose and the content of much of my conversation over the years. I am continually learning that the conversations of heaven are ready in an instant to tap into and release upon the earth—when my thinking is right.

Living How Heaven Lives

The journey of faith is the journey of life. And that life is full of tension. Tension between scared and liberation. Learning to live how heaven lives has perhaps been the most painful part of the journey as my teachers have primarily been illness and physical death.

It was a Matrix moment at the hinge point between despair and freedom in a doctor's chair where I saw how I had compartmentalized my life *and* my God. And it was staring into the face of a dying man outside Atlanta, Georgia on a rainy summer's night that revealed to me the metrics of life's success from heaven's perspective. There were two mighty powers at work that night in 1996; the triune God and my will. He won my heart with love. It had taken a long time, but I finally became authentic; relationally *real*.

A Final Word

Thinking, Speaking and Living. Life from heaven's perspective is what you are made for. Don't waste another day striving to live *toward* a place you have been designed to live *from*.

God has used many people and places to begin in me the transformation from unreal to real, a process that has eventually enabled me to think how heaven thinks, speak how heaven speaks, and live how heaven lives.

I can't become unreal again—why would I want to?

What about you?

The wooing of Holy Spirit is inviting you to live as a real part of the Bride of Christ from the position of heaven. He is wooing you into the fullness of that divine love relationship. He is causing this to happen all around you. Can you see it?

It is my firm belief as I travel this earth and converse with Kingdom marketplace leaders, that the next great revival to mark the pages of history will come through the marketplace. Decreasers and Policers doing the same things with a greater measure of intensity using performance metrics in natural strength will never bring that outcome about—it's not real. God has designed it such that only Kingdom Releasers who think how heaven thinks, speak how heaven speaks, and live how heaven lives can be the ones to write *those* pages of history.

I have sought to show you how you can think how heaven thinks, speak how heaven speaks, and live how heaven lives.

Now, I once more offer you an invitation. An invitation to access the new spiritual level revealed to you through these pages. It's your new position that reveals a new perspective. There will be times, while you think, speak and live like heaven, that you have a new encounter, a new thought, that will cause you to experience spiritual vertigo. I ask you, in those moments, to reach out and take Jesus' hand and keep going.

"Trust me. It is all good. It is amazing up here." This is Kingdom living—heaven to earth.

God is calling you to your true identity—A Releaser of the Kingdom of God! It's time to get real.

About the Author

Mark Appleyard grew up in Victoria Australia. For over twenty-years he has been involved in Christian leadership across the world that has included two church plants, turning a small church around to be a community impacting church as well as serving on the senior executive of a large multi-staff church in North Carolina.

Mark has served bi-vocationally for most of his ministry life, choosing for fifteen years to be in business on the east coast of Australia, while pastoring at a local level.

While still remaining founding pastor of Crossroads Church just outside of Charlotte North Carolina, Mark, along with his wife Julie, now also serve as founders of Anothen–a senior executive consulting network.

Anothen has been activated to fine tune Kingdom business leaders to think, speak and live from heaven's perspective–to help them become the most influential spiritual leaders in the world. Anothen has gained amazing momentum, and as of December 2016 is active daily in eight US states as well as ten nations.

With three grown children and a daughter in law, Mark and Julie Appleyard have dedicated their lives to bringing the nations as an inheritance to King Jesus by activating Kingdom people to "Think, Speak, Live" like heaven!

OTHER RESOURCES AVAILABLE

Thank you for purchasing
Think, Speak, Live, Business from Heaven's Perspective!

As part of our commitment to you, we invite you to
take advantage TODAY of our
FREE introductory offer:
a one-hour call with Mark.

Our desire is to help you become one of the most influential spiritual
leaders in the world.

To learn more about Mark and Julie Appleyard's work with Anothen,
and to access their other resources
or consultancy services:

Visit www.anothen.co

or simply scan the QR Code to get your FREE Introductory call!

www.anothen.co/get-started